ENTERTAINMENT DESTINATIONS

ENTERTAINMENT DESTINATIONS

MARTIN M. PEGLER

Visual Reference Publications • New York

Visual Reference Publications, Inc.
302 Fifth Avenue
New York, NY 10001

Distributors to the trade in the United States and Canada
Watson-Guptill
1515 Broadway
New York, NY 10036

Distributors outside the United States and Canada
HarperCollins International
10 East 53rd Street
New York, NY 10022-5299

Library of Congress Cataloging in Publication Data:
Entertainment Destinations

Printed in Hong Kong
ISBN 1-58471-012-8

Book Design: Dutton and Sherman

CONTENTS

INTRODUCTION

Why should anyone leave the house today looking for Entertainment? With TV screens becoming small movie screens, computers bringing the world into the home and turning dens into game arcades, cable connecting us to events as they occur and food only a phone call away—what out there can be so attractive? In order to lure people away from their home entertainment centers and into the world of fun/food and fashion—the trinity that makes most Entertainment Destinations entertainment destinations—developers, realtors and retailers have had to make everything bigger, bolder, brighter and more filled with brio and bombast to bring the pleasure seekers out.

Of course, you can watch a new movie on your home screen, courtesy of the local VCR rental store, for a lot less than tickets to the movies, but going out to the movies today is more like an adventure filled with amusement, amazement, glamour and glitz. With anywhere from a dozen to two or more dozen screens and movies to select from; with a variety of foods and refreshments available at the extravagant, neon-lit, 3D concessions; with game arcades for kids of all ages; and special areas for infants and party rooms—everything at home pales by comparison. These mega-cineplexes are becoming destinations in themselves or serving as anchors for entertainment centers. Theaters have always been entertainment destinations: from the Greek amphitheaters to the giant music halls and symphony centers. Here, again, food often comes with the experience and sometimes the thrill of shopping, even if only for souvenirs or memorabilia.

Think Entertainment: think Las Vegas! Think of gambling, game arcades, gala floor shows, gourmet restaurants. Think theme! But, Las Vegas is no longer the only game town—nor is gambling the only game in Vegas. Gameworks and family oriented amusement/ arcade centers like Coney Island Emporium and AdventureDome have arrived in Vegas and are thriving just as gaming is thriving in many parts of this country and abroad. In this book we touch on some casinos—from Atlantic City to Sydney, Australia and to amusement complexes from Sega City® The Playdium in Toronto to DisneyQuest in Puente Hills, CA.

Cruising has long been the ideal Entertainment Destination for many with the gigantic buffets of fine foods, gourmet treats, island hopping and tax-free shopping, to floating theaters big enough and fine enough to stage full scale musicals or concerts. Casinos float alongside the theaters in many sea- or ocean-going, five star, "boatels."

To some, sports and sporting events are what Entertainment is all about. With Chelsea Piers Sport/Entertainment Complex in NY and the All American SportPark in Las Vegas, we highlight and showcase these hot spots for sports and "personal perfection." We also show some of the "wellness centers" that combine exercise with socializing for trendy singles and families including children. For others, "mental gymnastics" is what fun is all about and Entros in Seattle and San Francisco come up with mind games/virtual reality and really good food and good times for thinking people—men and women. Billiards, once the game of low-lifes and "sharks" now swims in much more placid and, in some cases, more elegant waters like Kramer & Eugene's, Indian Motorcycle and that fun-for-all place up in Edmonton—Red's Rec Room. Dave & Buster's is sweeping across the country by providing fun and games and food—for the whole family.

We have only touched on some of the ever emerging and constantly developing Entertainment Destinations—the malls, centers and streets that are entirely devoted to the Entertainment concept. Some, like Topsy, keep growing and growing like the Entertainment Center at Irvine Spectrum. Some are new additions to existing malls much in need of a "draw" such as Denver Pavilions and Pacific Place. And some, like some of the above, are also helping to rejuvenate and revitalize urban areas that have been lost in time. Beale Street in Memphis and Clarke Quay in Singapore are two good examples of that trend.

It was true centuries ago when the emperors of Rome gave their masses "bread and blood" in the arenas to keep them happy, and it is even more true today when we give the people fun/food and fashions in colorful and energizing settings: "The world is a stage"—and that "stage" is very likely to be found in every Entertainment Destination.

Martin M. Pegler

ENTERTAINMENT DESTINATIONS

FAMOUS PLAYERS SILVER CITY

Toronto, ON, Canada

Design
International Design Group, Toronto, ON

Design Team
**Constanza Cursten / Ron Harris / Henrietta
Shenderey / Paules Ciskevicius**

Photography
Richard Johnson, Interior Images

This new design for Famous Players Silver City is located atop the Yonge & Englinton Centre in the heart of downtown Toronto. Rather than a free standing multiplex like the Mississauga project also shown in this edition, this is an in-city concept and differs from any other cineplex in the Famous Players chain.

The design is a happy and spirited blend of art deco and high tech which together affect the desired urban look. The designers have combined vivid colors, special dramatic and dynamic lighting effects and the TV monitors used to create an exciting and entertaining centre. The space is crowned by a "tornado" of fluorescent paints and neon trims "to reflect the energy and vitality of downtown Toronto."

From outside, through the vast curved glass windows set two streets above street level, the viewer on the street gets the sensation of swirling colors and light: a technicolor, out-of-space feeling. The large curved lobby area, inside, is filled with food concessions, tables and chairs, and lots of arcs, circles and undulating elements: floating neon-rimmed, plastic shapes and ribbon-like runners of wire covered with fine mesh. The main food concession is backed up with a replica of the famous Paramount Studio's arched opening gates. Blues, reds and yellow vinyl tiles are arranged on the floor to form a gigantic sunburst— adding to the celestial, out-of-this-world ambience of the lobby. ■

FAMOUS PLAYERS SILVER CITY

Mississauga, ON, Canada

Design
International Design Group, Toronto, ON

Design Team
**Ron Harris/Andrew Gallici/Jane
Graham/Donna Lawson/Paules
Ciskevicius/Brian Bettencourt**

Photography
Richard Johnson, Interior Images

The design challenge presented to the International Design Group of Toronto by Famous Players, a Canadian leader in motion picture entertainment, was to create a prototype theatre filled with exciting activities and services. Famous Players wanted a design that would "restore the fantasy and glamor" of theatres built earlier in the twentieth century.

The 60,000 sq. ft. theatre in Mississauga, ON can seat 3300 patrons in the state-of-the-art complex equipped with THX and digital sound. The designers prepared a bold package for the exterior, entrance and lobby to unite all the amenities and attractions. They specified a brilliant color palette of strong blues, vivid purples, reds, oranges and greens plus a plethora of eye-tingling patterns to "create an atmosphere of joie de vivre and vitality." Concentric patterning and wide stripes visually lead the patrons to the popcorn concession and the surrounding kiosks. The lobby layout uses a basic X/Y axis with the popcorn stand as its center point. The "Yum Yum Factory" is a configuration of overscaled gears, sprockets and sipping straws that sits atop the popcorn concession and serves as a beacon since it can be seen from anywhere in the "cinema street." This stand is framed by smaller, curved, specialty kiosks that are, in turn, crowned by a wavy, undulating bulkhead set 15 ft. off the floor in a space that soars to over 40 ft.

Durable materials were used throughout to withstand the wear and tear inflicted by the crowds of moviegoers. The laminated millwork has a glossy finish to "reinforce the overall con-

cept of an animated, playful interior." The seamless marmoleum flooring offers a large scale pattern with a virtually seamless appearance. Adding to the fun of the Famous Players Silver City experience are the Famous Cafe, NY Fries, Pizza Hut, and Tech Town filled with interactive games. Props and movie memorabilia such as, the F-14 fighter jet from "Top Gun" and the Flintmobile, pay tribute to the history, art and magic of the movies.

Lighting is used throughout to "deliver drama and punch." Spotlights, on the theatre exterior, scallop the building in beams that allude to the stucco pattern. Blue neon ribbons undulate around the lobby and they lead patrons to the assorted services and concessions. The retail areas are ablaze with halogen lights while theatrical light fixtures help to animate the props and memorabilia.

According to the designers, "Silver City Mississauga is a state-of-the-art movie palace, restoring for today's audiences the glamour and excitement of an older age.

"Uppermost in our minds was the need to create a warm, welcoming, fun environment that could appeal to everyone." Vibrant colors,, graphics, lighting and architecture are all imaginatively combined to create the energetic environment of this Famous Players Silver City. ■

AMC STUDIO THEATRES

Houston, TX

Design
Kiku Obata & Co., St. Louis, MO

Design Team
Kiku Obata/Kevin Flynn/Heather Testa/John Scheffel/Gen Obata/ Theresa Henrekin/James Keane/ Joe Floresvca/Liz Sullivan Lisa Bollman/Cliff Doucet/Carole Jerome/ Alissa Andres/Jonathan Bryant.

Architect (Shell)
Gould Evans Goodman, Kansas City, MO

Photography
Gary Quesada, Hedrick-Blessing, Chicago, IL

K iku Obata & Co. recently unveiled their newest design for the AMC Studio 30 Theatre in Houston, TX. It is "AMC's first and largest free standing theatre featuring a total entertainment environment." What the design attempts to do in the 110,000 sq. ft. space on a 23 acre plot is simulate a movie studio back lot and the sound stage where guests become part of the action and the experience "rekindles the magic and memory of movie going."

The 30,000 sq. ft. exterior courtyard is designed to reinforce the studio back lot atmosphere and the patrons are entering into the "sound stage." The patrons are encouraged to congregate in the entry plaza and enjoy the al fresco entertainment, music and food. Under the canopy and the marque lights the three box offices are located.

Inside, the balcony of the two level space provides the perfect place to see and be seen. Elements from sound stages and studio road cases make up the central lobby space along with a guest service desk. Images of Hollywood's glamorous stars of the past add enchantment to the balcony walls. The space is divided into three themed areas that "transport

guests into fantastic worlds of Animation, Action/Adventure and Cyberspace." The food concession stands within each area carries through the theme; "Fizz, Sizzle, Pop"; "Wildebeest Feast"; and "Quantum Bits." The 30 auditoria are located off the sound-stage lobby and within the various themed areas.

The architecture seems to come alive in the Animation area. The space is designed to resemble an animation cel: "flat, two-dimensional, cartoon-like graphics are outlined with black lines, filled with color and applied on an exaggerated scale." The Fizz, Sizzle, Pop concession's identity and blimp directional signs seem to float in a blue sky with flat, cut-out clouds.

The setting for Action/ Adventure recalls a rainforest with heavy hanging leaves, bamboo and rock "carved" directional signs. The custom wall covering features petroglyphs of cave people carrying popcorn, megaphones and movie cameras. The fiber optic eyes peering from behind the leaves in the Wildebeest Feast stand change color. They also appear above rock outcroppings down the corridor.

Patrons are invited to explore an abstract, futuristic world in Cyberspace where the floor and ceiling are the same color and brushed alu-

minum columns rise partway to the ceiling. To create the illusion of "endless space." custom light fixtures project beams of light along the walls and backlit graphic images have neon edges. Various colored lights and a high-tech fluorescent green/orange acrylic sign help to define the Quantum Bits concession area in Cyberspace.

According to the designers," AMC Studio 30 treats its guests to a total entertainment event. The prototype's appeal to all age groups, its ability to integrate retail, food and guests' services and its flexibility as a community forum for corporate use, live broadcasting or expanded viewing is redefining the motion picture exhibition industry." ■

AMC ONTARIO
MILLS 30

**Ontario Mills Mall,
Ontario, CA**

Architectural Design/Architect of Record
**Salts, Troutman, Kaneshiro,
San Jacinto, CA**

Project Manager
Camille Acton

Themimg & Interior Design/Environmental
Graphics
GB Design, Kansas City, MO

Project Coordinator
Roger A. Reed

Designer (graphics)
Chris Nobrega

Photography
Jim Baker, Foto Designs, Kansas City, MO

With 30 screens, AMC Ontario Mills becomes the world's largest theatre and that makes a statement! When that "statement" is written out in bold colors, rich materials and dynamic Hollywood style lighting effects,—it is a very dramatic statement.

The theatre also serves as an identity marker for the entrance to the entertainment complex at the Ontario Mills Mall. The cinema's facade of rough cut stone, stucco and a metal panel system comes alive under the iridian building illuminators that change color by means of an electronic, programmed color palette. The box office, which is brought out into the courtyard, is highlighted by a huge illuminated globe that seems to float over it. The globe appears to hover and rotate and the 28 high power, 150-watt halide illuminator

and hundreds of feet of fiber optic cable all help to achieve that effect. Internally illuminated Kalwall columns lead to the entry and perched on a canopy over the doors is a 15 ft. interactive video entertainment system (L.I.V.E.). It provides promotional information and entertains the patrons by playing trailers of upcoming attractions.

The lobby is a wide space highlighted with playful sculptures, rich colors and textures, and exciting lighting effects. The AMC logo, in neon script, the backlit plexiglass panels and the TV monitors provide "a colorful interplay between the various lobby features and the signage beyond." The sculptural elements are ringed with neon to suggest "portholes to outer space" and they are made even more dramatic by the use of Wildfire UV activated paints and the strategically placed black lights.

The assorted individual auditoria combine full stadium seating with wide aisles, great sight lines, and improved acoustics which prevent sound from bleeding through from one auditorium to another. The theatres are equipped with high back seats with retractable arm rests that can convert into "love seats." Torrus screens are used. They are vacuum formed, curved screens which tilt up to better match the projector's curved lens thus creating less distortion. Throughout the cinema the custom designed signage is internally illuminated to clearly identify phones, restrooms and the thirty auditoria. ■

EDWARDS 21 CINEMAS

**Irvine Spectrum,
Irvine, CA**

Design
**Perkowitz + Ruth Architects,
Long Beach, CA**

Photography
**A.G. Photography/Perkowitz + Ruth
Architects**

The Edwards 21 Cinemas—complete with 3D Imax—opened only a few years ago in the Retail/Entertainment center, Irvine Spectrum. At the time of its inauguration, this multiplex was the largest multiplex in the U.S. and "the epitome of the new standard."

Designed by Perkowitz + Ruth, Inc. of Long Beach who have since then produced many other noteworthy cinemas for the Edwards Chain, it set a format that, with variations to suit a particular audience or neighborhood, has proven extremely successful. "The experience begins at the sidewalk." says Simon Perkowitz, CEO of the architectural firm, "with grand and glittering marquees and spectacular landscaping beckoning customers to glamourous lobbies and into sumptuous, interactive theatres exhibiting an awesome display of technical wizardry."

The entranceway to this cinema complex is truly a "grand gateway" asizzle with neon and lights, interesting forms and attractive colors. It is designed as a large rotunda to create an impressive visual experience and to reflect, in contemporary vernacular, the famous and now mostly gone movie palaces of the 1920s and 1930s.

Inside, the lobby is a soaring and dramatic space that measures 96 ft. wide and encompasses an area of 15,000 sq. ft. Rather than a movie house, the interior feels like the lobby in a performing arts or opera house center.

The theatre is decorated with many different imported marbles, vibrant murals, dramatic, sweeping staircases and art deco inspired trim of stainless steel and brass. There are exquisitely designed and crafted mosaic tile floors and more than three miles of neon lighting set the space ablaze. The individual auditoria range in seating capacity from 200 to 1200. Stadium-style seating

allows unobstructed views of the screen and the moveable arm rests give patrons the option of turning their seats into a "screening environment complete with couches."

The 3D Imax theatre features a screen large enough to project a life-size image of a whale on 135mm film format. Added to this is the 80 speaker, six digit sound system which is enhanced by an additional pair of sound channels (transducers) built into each viewer's personal headset which provides the 3D sound to complement the picture. Again, quoting Simon Perkowitz, "Using more holistic approaches as they emerge as centerpieces of new urban shopping experiences, motion picture theatres have become entertainment destinations that recognize the common public yearning for gathering places and communal experiences." ∎

UCI HUDDERSFIELD CINEMA

Cardiff Bay, UK

Design
Fitch, London, UK

Photography
Courtesy Fitch

The 12 screen UCI Cinema in Huddersfield, Cardiff Bay not only boasts of the largest movie screen in the UK (16.9 m x 7.2 m) but also represents the new generation of cinema design. There is not only state-of-the-art technology used in different movie viewing areas but the complex includes a retail shop for movie related merchandise, a popcorn bar, a pick'n'mix candy section, a game arcade and a Ben & Jerry's Ice Cream Cafe.

Through the contributions of Universal and Paramount studios, the parent company of UCI Cinemas, "cinema-scale" illuminated images, giant posters, montages and supergraphic word walls "capture classic moments and famous quotes" from well known movies of the past. These decorative elements cover the space within the ticket area, main foyer, retail shop, cafe, bar and the children's party room.

The three level, glass fronted theatre has the ticket counter at ground level: the main foyer and nine auditoria are on the first level up. A themed "movie bar" is situated on the top level. The bar/lounge draws upon west coast glamour and the sophistication of Hollywood for its inspiration. There is a screen size image of Robert DeNiro and a Hitchcock "heritage wall" as definitive "stay-around" motivators for the cinema audience. The lounge also is an entertainment destination for non movie goers.

In one of the auditoria, the designers have introduced the "black box" concept. Since the only illumination in the theatre is from the nosing lights on the stairs, the environment is totally blacked out while the film is being projected. It "creates a uniquely magical viewing environment." Most of the auditoria, however, are designed and executed in red with the exception of the aforementioned "black box" where the seats, walls, ceiling and floor are all black. The 12 auditoria have stadium seating and Dolby digital sound. The largest auditorium has a 15m x 6.5m screen and a 500 seat capacity.

"Such an approach to cinema design destroys the commonplace threshold between the enjoyment of films inside the auditoria and the relative anonymity of the adjoining multiplex space, to create a seamless cinematic sensation. In short, Fitch and UCI have conceived cinema going as an holistic entertainment experience." ∎

MUVICO "DRIVE-IN" THEATER

Pompano Beach, FL

Architect & Graphic Design
**Development Design Group,
Baltimore, MD**

Themed Element Fabrication
RCC, Inc., Miami, FL

Photography
Development Design Group, Baltimore, MD

As we enter the new millennium we keep turning back to look at "the good old days" with more and more fondness—and with a bit of envy. In the movies we go back to "Pleasantville" and only laugh a little at what was, just as Generation X-ers and even some of the Baby Boomers tune in to Nickelodeon to recapture the times when "Father Knows Best" and we could "Leave it to Beaver." What could be more natural than to recapture some of that nostalgia in one of the ultimate entertainment experiences of the 1950s—the Drive-In movie.

The 71,000 sq. ft., 18 screen Muvico Theatre designed by Development Design Group of Baltimore reflects our love affair with the good old days. Inspired by and using motifs of that period, the theatre, located in Pompano Beach, FL, is rich in the bold geometric patterns and the primary color palette that is usually associated with the vintage drive-in movies. The facade is a vibrant composition of red, white and blue with a red and gold gigantic movie reel unwinding atop a red metal pylon. "Muvico 18" appears in a blue "ribbon" of film strip that forms the opening arch over the entrance into the movie house. The ticket counter is playfully based on an old style radio case and other themed motifs are introduced inside the lobby. There are juke-box style revolving poster cases, classic cars sliced in half

and facing a giant "screen" with animatronic waitresses and "trunk" seats for phone booths. 1950-ish road side signs, rich in color and neon, appear throughout—like the "motel" sign that designates the game arcade/video game area. The Hot Spot Grill is readily located under a monster steaming coffee cup and the checkerboard patterned backup elements. The concessions area gets an extra dollop of light and color along with a huge framed, changing billboard.

Along with its fun theme and colorful setting, the 18 screen theatre also boasts of the most state-of-the-art technology in seating, sound and projection in the individual auditoria which can accommodate up to 3400 patrons. ■

MUVICO PARADISE 24 THEATER

Davie, FL

Design, Architecture & Graphics
**Development Design Group,
Baltimore, MD**

Theme Element Fabrication
Renwal, Rancho Cucamonga, CA

Photography
Muvico Theatres, Ft. Lauderdale, FL

The 8500 sq. ft. multiplex cinema recently opened in Davie, FL was almost immediately ranked in the top five grossing theatres per capita in the U.S. With the architectural and graphics design by Development Design Group of Baltimore, this 24 screen movie house can seat over 4000 patrons.

The inspiration for the Paradise 24 is so old that it is new again. Like the great movie palaces that were built in the 1920s and 1930s, the Paradise is based on an historic theme. Instead of slavishly following the details of the periods past, this rendition brings it up to date and affords the patrons a glimpse of what was in a crisp, new and contemporary way. The facade resembles that of an Egyptian temple with giant lotus capped columns and mammoth sloping masonry walls. The north wing of the cinema complex is reminiscent of the sandy, desert-oriented upper Nile, while the southern wing is themed as a much more lush Delta plain. Colossal Ramses-like statues guard the concession stand which is located at the end of an outdoor/indoor mosaic of the Nile river.

The interior appears vast with giant hieroglyphic inscribed columns forming a grid within the space. Rings of light illuminate the stylized lotus caps atop the columns. The ceiling is coffered with a blue wash "sky" appearing between the criss-crossing bands of masonry.

Throughout, the designers have used the ancient Egyptian vocabulary of decorative elements to enhance the experience. There are colorful fascias of Egyptian styled figures over the individual auditoria entrances, and the architectural portal to each theatre resembles some ancient mastaba prototype. In keeping with the theme, historic names are inscribed on each of the twenty-four auditoria. In addition to the cafe and the concession facility, there is also a video game arcade and a playroom for the smaller children. ■

SONY'S STAR THEATRE

Southfield, MI

Design
Rockwell Group, New York, NY

Photography
Paul Warchol, New York, NY

The new flagship Star Theatre, designed by the noted "entertainment" designer David Rockwell and the Rockwell Group of New York is a 170,000 sq. ft. facility with 20 auditoria ranging from 100 to 700 seats and four restaurants. The inspiration for the design is Hollywood of the 1930s and it is interpreted on the exterior with a streamlined art deco design. At night, with the use of colored lights, the warm gold and red colored areas are complemented by the cool blue washes of light behind the walls and towers constructed of glass blocks. The swirls, loops and sweeps that extend out to the sign overhanging the street are recognizable as 1930s motifs.

"Once inside, the visitor is transported to our interpretation of a 1930s Hollywood set," in the Hollywood Blvd. lobby. The lobby is complete with sweeping arches, palm trees, and "stage set" theatrical renditions of shop fronts and theatre facades. The center lobby has a concession stand that features bubbling "soda" columns and a colossal popcorn bucket overflowing with kinetically popping popcorn. Overscaled reels of film with memorable movie scenes unspool and wrap around the stylized boom movie cameras.

Movie flats line the walls and hang from the ceiling amid the pulleys, catwalks, and sandbags in the "Sound Stage Lobby." The third lobby in this Star Cinema pays tribute to the historic people, monuments and architecture of nearby Detroit. Video Games are integrated into this "sepia colored walk through memory lane." ■

CINESCAPE

Calgary, AB, Canada

Design
Shikatani Lacroix Design, Inc., Toronto, ON

President
Jean Pierre Lacroix

Project Managers
Edward Shikatani/Jean Pierre Lacroix

Design Team
Lynn Giles/Eric Boulden/Janet Jones/Zaiba Mian/Beverly Wells

Project Architect
The Coho Evamy Partners

Photography
John Narvali, Toronto, ON

The design challenge for Shikatani Lacroix of Toronto started with an 18,000 sq. ft. warehouse adjacent to Cineplex's Eau Clair Market Cinema in Calgary. The design firm was invited to transform the space into an entertainment venue which would house high tech, interactive game technology, visual reality games, animated video attractions, Internet stations, billiard tables, a giant TV screen plus a 250 seat restaurant/cafe/bar. Using revolutionary design concepts, this prototype design evolved which "showcases the latest in entertainment technology in the world."

"Our objective was to create an environment that would draw guests into the space and appeal to their senses. We achieved this primarily through the use of color and creating a sense of movement that engages and guides the guests as they explore the many entertainment stations," said Jean Pierre Lacroix of the design firm. Lighting and lighting effects were used to define the various spaces and activities thus "creating stations with an individual appeal." The intensity of the illumination, in many

areas, can be varied. Clear lights are focused on the walls and spotlights are used to highlight the individual games. The overall effect of Cinescape is one of "cinematic excitement, interest, and magic without being busy or cluttered." Adjustable acoustic blankets in the ceiling, wall panels and modular panels in the restaurant were all incorporated to facilitate the inevitable expansion of the project.

With careful attention to design and color integration, bold sharp colors, and themed neon signage played against a theatrical black background, Cinescape is a class act for Cineplex Odeon and a dramatic showcase for the design talents of Shikatani Lacroix. ■

SEGA STATION ARCADE

Kansas City, MO

Design
Kiku Obata & Co., St. Louis, MO

Design Team
Kiku Obata/Kevin Flynn, AIA/Anselmo Testa, AIA/Cliff Doucet/Nao Etsuki/Kathleen Robert/Arden Powell/Matt McInerny

Photography
Gary Quesada, Clawson, MI

Kiku Obata and Co., a St. Louis design firm, designed the futuristic flight into time and space setting for the Sega Station Arcade in the Station Casino in Kansas City, MO. Kevin Flynn, of the design team, said, "The video arcade is based on a colorful world of futuristic trains and travel," befitting the location in this historic renovated train station. To create the dynamic environment that simulates the fast paced energy of the video games, the designers used bright colors, moving lights, bold graphics and angular shapes.

The space is divided into two distinct areas of play. There is the hot and stimulating area for video games that the teenagers throng to and in the other area the games are scaled down for younger children. They can win tickets that can be redeemed for prizes at the Redemption Center. The two areas are separated by garage doors that pull down . They feature strong, fun and colorful graphics. Adding to the entertainment of the Sega Station Arcade are the out-of-this-world train station platform, over scaled travel tags from faraway and exotic places as well as three dimensional, futuristic motor wheels that seem to spin—adding even more energy to the already kinetic environment. The strong, bright colors, sharp angular lines and the blast of sparkling and flashing lights all add to the play experience in the arcade. ■

GAMEWORKS

Las Vegas, NV

Design
Cuningham Group, Los Angeles, CA

Principal in Charge
Jim Sheidel, AIA

Project Manager
Jonathan Wate, AIA

Design Team
Tracy Wade/Mike Predergast/Shaun Jennings/Pauline Lyders

Interior Design Team
Tom Bolin, CID/Jan Dufault, CID/Jim Lewison, CID

For GAMEWORKS

Project Manager
Tim Sepielle

Director of Design Production
Jim Scheiter

Sr. Concept Designer
Stuart Bailey

Photography
Eric Sander, Ronald Moore & Associates

A new concept in night club environment that offers the best in technology, games and social interaction is currently on view in Las Vegas. It is GameWorks—a new entertainment experience—and this prototype design was created by the Cuningham Group for this new venture that brings together Dreamworks, Sega Enterprises and Universal Studios. It is estimated that by the year 2002 there will be 100 GameWorks around the world.

Located in the Showcase on the Las Vegas strip, this 47,000 sq. ft. flagship is laid out on two levels and it includes interactive games specially designed by Steven Spielberg of Dreamworks. Part of the entertainment is access to the Internet, a free standing rock climbing structure and food and beverage areas. The designers took their inspiration from a make-believe Victorian warehouse where, as the "script" would have it—"weird events and strange, often alien experiments" were being conducted. Jonathan Watts, associate and project manager for GameWorks said, "Essentially, the facility becomes a stage for this story and guests fill in the script."

The lower level game floor is flooded with high energy colors, rich textures and dramatic lighting effects. The entrance or street level—The Loft— is a quieter gathering/socializing space with reused warehouse wood flooring that adds to the warm and friendly feeling of this space. Tom Bolin, Director of Interior Design for the Cuningham Group said,"This is where we chose to specify reused materials in order to create a lived-in effect. There's a comfortable leather couch, the oversized draperies are velvet and the lighting is softer."

A newer version of the GameWork project follows. ■

GAMEWORKS

The Streets of Woodfield, Schaumberg, IL

Design
Sr.V.P. of Design for GameWorks:
Jon Snoddy

Photography
Courtesy of GameWorks

"As kids we loved watching computer games explode onto the scene and loved going to arcades. But, when we grew up, the arcades did not. At GameWorks; we're building the entertainment concept that closes the gap and gives adults and kids (young or old) the ultimate place to play," said Skys Paul, Chairman and co-founder of GameWorks. Working with Steven Spielberg, they concocted a place where "people of all ages can play and interact in dramatically themed neighborhoods."

GameWorks is about having fun. Steven Spielberg says, "Playing is about fun, excitement, competition and bringing people together. It's about adventure and connecting. It gives each person the chance to prove that he or she can be a star."

GameWorks is a joint venture of Dreamworks, Sega Enterprises and Universal Studios. The concept is that "Life's a game and it's meant to be played." And it's about games, drinks, music, food and friends. It is designed to be an entertainment destination where adults and families can play eat, drink and socialize in signature zones that offer a variety of high intensity, visually stimulating and relaxing experiences. By day, friends and business associates can meet for lunch and relax with a variety of motion simulation games. At night the mood and atmosphere changes. It becomes "an adult destination."

GameWorks is divided into a series of "neighborhood environments"—each with its own per-

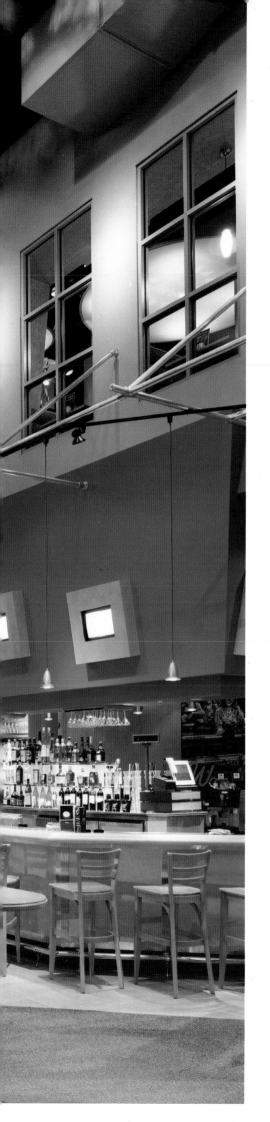

sonality defined by the design, lighting, color and sound. The Entertainment Zones can be high energy—visually stimulating—or relaxing. The Loading Dock is a high-energy zone where the newest games are "unloaded from the delivery truck" and put to the test at once by hard core, game enthusiasts. The Arena features the signature games designed exclusively for GameWorks. They mix the high-tech thrills of video games with the visceral excitement of theme-park style attractions. The Grill & Bar features a sit-down restaurant where guests can enjoy a meal or a "cool down" between games. There is also a snack bar and some venues feature bars with beer brewed on site.

The 34,000 sq. ft. GameWorks at Streets of Woodfield in Schaumberg, IL features Virtual Reality, Indy 500 racing, a Max Flight VR2002 Roller Coaster, a virtual arena as well as a variety of high energy, motion simulation games. Virtual Reality is "the most intense game play imaginable in which players experience physical consequences based on their skill level." Eight players can "race head to head on the Indy 500 motion simulator game." Guests can plan their own "space trips" on the Max Flight VR2002 Roller Coaster. Once strapped in, the traveler is propelled skyward and does the exact same back flips, spins and loops as those being projected on the 58 in. screen.

In an article that appeared in Shopping Center World, Randall Shearin wrote, "GameWorks continues to be one of the most innovative concepts around and definitely one of the most colorful. And, by far, it is definitely still the most sought after entertainment in the world." At this time there are more than a dozen GameWorks in operation across the U.S., and into Guam and Brazil. ■

ADVENTUREDOME

**Circus Circus Hotel/Casino,
Las Vegas, NV**

Photography
Courtesy of Circus Circus Hotel/Casino

In a glass covered construction, under the sunny or starry skies of Las Vegas, the AdventureDome is located. It is a major family entertainment attraction of the Circus Circus Hotel/Casino property. Billed as "America's largest indoor theme park," the AdventureDome is filled with fun and excitement, rides and games and thrills galore all in a Southwest themed environment designed to recall the colors and textures of the Grand Canyon.

Included in the roster of thrill rides is the "breath-taking, double loop, double corkscrew Canyon Blaster roller coaster" which seems to soar, dip, fly and swirl through, up and down the craggy, man-made mountains inside the AdventureDome. There is also the Rim Runner boat ride where the brave and hearty can plummet down a 60 ft. waterfall or the "demented clown chaos" that emanates from the nutty, funny Fun House Express ride which is an Imax Ridefilm that utilizes motion simulator technology. For team laser tag enthusiasts, there is Hot Shots and in the Xtreme Zone thrill seekers can climb walls or bounce in the air on a Bungee Trampoline. In addition to the midway games and the high tech arcade games, for the younger visitors there is the Mystic Magic Theater, a Fossil Dig, a Dinosaur Habitat and a host of scaled-down rides. These include a full size carousel, bumper cars and more activities where parents can either accompany the children or watch from within camera range.

The AdventureDome's dome-like enclosure is made up of over 8500 panes of glass and each pane weighs in at over 300 pounds. AdventureDome was ranked in the top 25 American theme parks listed by the Amusement Business Magazine. ∎

CONEY ISLAND EMPORIUM

New York/New York Hotel, Las Vegas, NV

Design
Haverson Architecture & Design, Greenwich, CT

Photography
Paul Warchol

The New York/New York Hotel/Casino stands strong and draws throngs to its Las Vegas Blvd. location in the theme-oriented city of Las Vegas. Outside, in a reduced scale, the architects and designers of NY/NY have encapsulated the architecture and excitement of NYC and inside—in the assorted areas of the hotel/casino complex—the theming goes on.

Coney Island Emporium "is a colorful maze of amusement park amenities, set in a magical wonderland of excitement, fun, and adventure." There is the illusion of the thrilling roller coaster ride high above a boardwalk that is made real by the intermittent screaming sound effects that burst into the carefree ambience. You can hear bumper cars collide, and mushrooming up, overhead, is the parachute jump. To help keep the wonderful and wholesome feeling of a bye-gone era when a trip to Coney Island was what a trip to Disneyland is today, the designers, Haverson Architecture & Design of Greenwich, CT blew up vintage post cards of the original Coney Island boardwalk in its heyday. There are also old-fashioned images of people playing or strolling on the beach. These enlarged views "imbued with color and clever eye-catching graphics encourage visitors to step back in time."

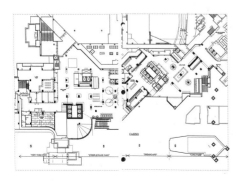

The meandering boardwalk features a "colossal show" of rides, shooting galleries, and game arcades filled with the latest games including virtual reality games, laser tag and ride simulations. All of these are to satisfy the most demanding thrill requirements of this 21st century generation. Interspersed are more "old fashioned" games which are designed "to conjure up child-like expectations of winning a prize." To get to all of this excitement, the visitor gets onto "the subway" and in almost a flash is set down in this NY NY fun area. From here they have access to The Tunnel of Love and simulations of the famous Steeplechase and Luna Park—landmarks of Coney Island's halcyon days.

This 32,000 sq. ft. family entertainment space was the inspiration of Michael Getlan, Dir. Of Operations for Amusement Consultants who saw the possibilities of adding Coney Island Emporium to the overall NY flavor of NY NY. In this 24 hour arcade there is the aroma of cotton candy and candy apples; the sound of gun shots and squealing tires and one can't help but inhale deeply the fragrant aroma emanating from the Nathan's hot-dog stand where hot dogs and french fries head the menu.

According to the designers, "Unique places of fun and relaxation, the themed settings when creatively conceived, can be tantamount to a magical getaway, a nostalgic reprieve from the reality of the world as we know it." Coney Island Emporium provides a fun ride back to the good old days when the world seemed brighter and happier. ■

DISNEYQUEST®

Walt Disney World Resort™
Orlando, FL

Design
**Walt Disney Imagineering & Disney
Regional Entertainment**

Photography
Courtesy of the Walt Disney Company

The first DisneyQuest®, a five story, indoor, interactive theme park, opened recently in Walt Disney World Resort!™ in Orlando, FL. It combines Disney's magic with cutting edge immersive technologies such as virtual reality to provide excitement and entertainment for guests of all ages. Art Levitt, Disney Regional Entertainment's president said, DisneyQuest® is "a place filled with virtual

adventure that puts you in the middle of the experience. With a two or three hour visit, families will be able to embark on adventures that allow them to actually 'enter the story' and become part of it".

Some of the adventures that await visitors to DisneyQuest® include a ride aboard a real river raft—or the thrill of paddling and shooting the rapids while on a virtual cruise through the jungle. Guests can ride a roller coaster of their own design on Cyberspace Mountain or "descend" into Hades where they can help Hercules and his friends battle the forces of evil. Take a ride on Aladdin's Magic Carpet and soar over the streets of Agrabah. These are only a few of the breathtaking experiences created by Walt Disney Imagineering, the Company's R & D and theme park design group. Joe Di Nuzio, V.P. of new ventures of Walt Disney Imagineering said, "We saw this concept as a tremendous challenge. I am confident we have succeeded in creating an entirely new kind of entertainment experience for our guests".

Visitors begin their journey of discovery at Ventureport. From there they can take off into any of the distinct entertainment environments:

The Explore Zone (a virtual adventure land filled with exotic and ancient locales); The Score Zone (a superhero competition city where guests can match their game-playing skills against the best); The Create Zone (a private "imagineering studio" for artistic self-expression); and The Replay Zone (a retro-futuristic, carnival-on-the-moon, setting where classic rides and games are presented with a new and novel twist.).

The Cheesecake Factory Express provides a "quick gourmet fix" in two separate areas—FoodQuest and Wonderland Cafe. A one-of-a-kind retail shop, also in DisneyQuest®, is filled with fun mementos of the visit.

"Coming to a city near you"—are some new DisneyQuest® Entertainment Centers. The Chicago store, on Rush and Ohio, has recently opened and due in 2000 is the Philadelphia center which will serve as an anchor to the Pavilion at Market East. This is a new development which will feature family oriented entertainment, a multiplex movie theatre and other retail and restaurant attractions.

Other family-oriented Entertainment Destinations under the banner of Disney Regional Entertainment are: ESPN Zone®, a sports-themed dining and entertainment venue in Baltimore, Chicago and in New York's Times Square as well as Club Disney® family "playsites" in Southern California, Phoenix and the Denver area. ■

MALIBOU
SPEED ZONE

Puente Hills, CA

Design
ID8/RTKL

VP in Charge
Jeff Gunning

Project Manager
Randy McCown

Int. Design & Theming
Andra Newsom

Graphic Arts
Mark Askew

Photography
Craig Blackman

The prototype for Malibou Speed Zone, a racing theme park, was designed by ID8—the entertainment and theme design division of RTKL Associates. They provided the architectural, interior and graphic designs.

The 287,000 sq. ft. park "responds to America's demand for unique entertainment experiences," said Jeff Gunning, AIA, who was the VP in charge of designing this project. Themed around auto racing with tracks that range from formula one to high speed dragster attractions, the park is detailed so that visitors become totally immersed in the experience. "The atmosphere takes on a life of its own—it's a simultaneous equation of space, light, color, motion—and most of all—speed."

The patterns, colors and forms are all derived from racing iconography. The wavy roofed, shade structures scattered throughout the park along with the central ticket kiosk tower and the series of venue gateways and service buildings all are clustered around the central clubhouse building. The Clubhouse is designed with a highway-scaled, front end of a race car as the park facade while the back of the car becomes the parking lot facade. Inside, the car facade runs through the center as a unifying element. To either side are high tech games and a redemption center. The Speed Zone Cafe, a

retail area dubbed "Parts Department," as well as private function rooms and administration services are located here. The upper wall area—over the bar—carries a giant mural of speed racing cars and it is repeated "at billboard scale" on the building exterior "to become the signature image of the park."

Within the park there are four tracks and four different types of cars. Included are: Top Eliminator Dragsters; Slik Trax; Grand Prix; and Turbo Track. In addition, in this family entertainment center which appeals to young adults and families "who love the thrill of speed," there is a 30-hole miniature golf course which is also designed around the racing theme.

The design was created as "a kit of parts" so that it could be adapted to varying real estate opportunities including spaces inside malls. "The basic design," according to Jeff Gunning," is there for two reasons: ease of construction and consistency of image."

"It's that recognizable imagery which is intended to create identity for the Malibou name: the buildings and the shade structures are all part of that brand." ∎

JEEPERS!

Rockville, MD

Design
FRCH Design Worldwide, New York, NY

Photography
George Cott, Tampa, FL

To make a bolder presence and create a more inviting venue, FRCH Design Worldwide was commissioned by Jungle Jim Playlands, Inc.—a chain of family entertainment centers—to design a completely new prototype that would help them to achieve their desired goals in the increasingly competitive market.

The 26,000 sq. ft. facility, first opened in Rockville, MD and since then rolled out in multiple locations, is a mini theme park with rides and games for children ages two to 12. It also includes separate areas for live shows, private parties, and soft play dates. "With its over-the-top, cartoon inspired design, Jeepers! bombards the senses with visual stimulation and sets the stage for a fun filled outing for the entire family."

Rather than investing heavily in architectural elements, the designers developed a graphics based solution that relies heavily on "elaborate theming, enjoying cartoony characters, catchy names and a host of cost effective design elements." They used bright and bold colors, startling textures, weird and wonderfully eccentric shapes, vivid patterns and theatrical lighting to create the jungle imagery. A family of characters was developed to give the space a much needed layer of personality. Featured throughout the energetic and kinetic space are J.J. the Monkey, Kronkle his sidekick and Trish the tiny rhino. They are also brought to life by actors who dress up in the character's costumes for special events and parties.

Focal points are strategically placed for greatest impact. To heighten the excitement and establish a distinct identity for each attraction, elaborate portals are set in front of the zones and rides. Mostly the effects were produced with painted gypsum wall board and stained

strand board. The design team also devised attractive and fun names for the various attractions like Tarantula Tangle for a scrambler and Banana Squadron for a Red Baron "plane" ride. Kids that want to do bumper cars must enlist in the J.J.Driving School. Pizza Hut's food service is now Tiny Rhino Diner where the 1950-ish design complements the child-oriented happy food menu.

The staging area for live entertainment takes place in a "tree house" where J.J. and his friends put on mini performances, magic acts or puppet shows. The shows are simultaneously shown on TV monitors throughout the entertainment space.

The design team's efforts also extended to theming the employee uniforms, collateral material and creating an array of branded merchandise that is sold in Jeepers! Following the success of this design, a scaled-down version called Jeepers Jr! will open in select Toys'R'Us Kids World stores. ■

SEGA CITY®
THE PLAYDIUM

Toronto, ON, Canada

Design
II X IV Design Associates, Toronto, ON

Architect
Kuwabarp Payne McKenna Blumberg

Photography
David Whittaker, Toronto

"We want to use technology to provide the quality and thrills of Disneyland in a small space," said Hayao Nayakama, President of Sega Enterprises, Ltd. In a joint venture Toronto's Playdium Enterprises, Sega Enterprises U.S. along with the design know-how of the Toronto design firm, II X IV Design Associates, came up with this innovative new entertainment destination for young adults and families.

The 36,000 sq. ft., trapezoidal shaped building which houses the Sega City Interactive Entertainment Center, anchors a 12 acre amusement complex which includes a go-cart course, miniature golf course and an indoor-outdoor baseball academy. Guests pass through the "jaws" of a giant sliding steel doorway decorated with the Sega City® The Playdium logo. They walk along a "space bridge"—an expanse of heavy glass illuminated from above and below. The bridge is suspended away from the perimeter walls which are pitted and cratered to simulate a lunar landscape. Heaps of "moonrocks" glow under the UV lighting that emanates from the arched, buttress-like ribs that extend up from the tunnel walls. Guests pass through and trigger off light and motion sensors and a range of special effects. At the SFX tunnel exit there is an information wall and a way-finding system.

The walls and ceilings are painted a deep blue-purple while the floors are laid with gray, charcoal and black marmoleum tiles and carpet. Reinforced fiberglass with a highly reflective opalescent finish transforms 11 giant structural columns into "strangely undulating shapes interrupted by protruding acrylic horns," and they are topped with mushroom caps lined with cracked mirrors.

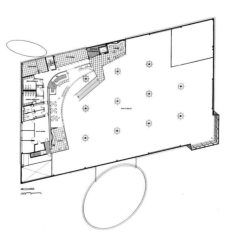

67

The individual play zones are clearly recognizable and they are entered through 14 ft. archways that are elaborately constructed to indicate the nature of the activity beyond the archway. They can be anything from rocket ships to Indy 500 finish line flags. Sega's virtual games and rides are in The Simulation Zone and The Fight Zone is devoted to martial arts play. Golf simulators, a golf school and air hockey are housed in The Sports Zone. The eight person Virtual Formula interactive ride, small Daytonas units and a four person motorcycle racing game can be found in The Racing Zone. The elevated Flight Zone features flight simulators. In the IMAX Ridefilm Theater guests can enjoy the latest in motion simulator rides

In each zone noted above appropriate lighting and video images are projected on the walls. The Retail Zone was designed with riveted, galvanized tile units that resemble early images of Sci-Fi space ships and mobile "moon buggies" appear on the selling floor to display featured merchandise. This area also serves as the Information Center, handles pre-ticket sales, function room bookings, and as the Redemption Center for prizes.

Tucked away under the mezzanine with a lower ceiling and a more child-like scale is The Kids Zone. Here the animated and colorful backdrops create a fantastic cityscape with "a crazy quilt of building facades in vivid polka dots, plaids and stripes."

Overlooking the gaming floor are two bar/lounge areas, a series of party rental rooms and an Internet lounge. In this space, on custom modular sofas, "circles" of up to four persons can face individual monitors.

The Sega City® The Playdium environment was created to appeal to a wide age group. It "expresses different personalities at different times for different purposes: brighter and more colorful during the day and more dimly lit and dramatic in the later evening". ■

STAR TREK: THE EXPERIENCE

Las Vegas Hilton, Las Vegas, NV

Design
Architect of Record: The Cuningham Group, Minneapolis, MN

Executive Producer & Developer
Paramount Parks

Sr. Creative Consultant
Rick Berman

Design Consultant
Herman Zimmerman

Sr. VP Design & Development
Anthony Esparza

Attraction Producer
Landmark Entertainment Group

Photography
Gary Zee, Opulence Studios, Inc.

S tar Trek: The Experience is an interactive adventure based on the fantastic voyages of the futuristic TV series Star Trek. Visitors to this joint venture between Paramount Parks and the Las Vegas Hilton are "immersed in a futuristic world where they see, feel, touch and live in the 24th century."

A visit to the 65,000 sq. ft. entertainment attraction starts with a visit to the StarQuest casino. A giant portal, at the end of the themed casino, opens onto a view of models of the USS Enterprise, Bird of Prey and the USS Enterprise 1-701-D—suspended from the ceiling against a deep sky wall filled with thousands of flickering stars. A ramp leads to the ticket sales booth—and the adventure truly begins. Soon, the guests are "beamed" aboard the Starship Enterprise. On the bridge of the airship, an exact recreation of the TV set familiar to millions, guests become part of a Star Trek adventure and "the future of the universe lies in their hands." After a dramatic ride on the Turbo Lift to the Grand Corridor (never actually shown in the TV series), the space travelers are escorted to the shuttle craft bay where they board a

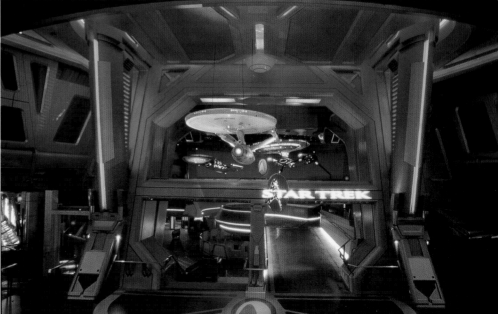

27-seat shuttle craft for "the ultimate journey through Star Trek universe."

The motion simulator ride has been developed using a new "immersive" viewer tilt perspective and the riders are completely out of touch with the "real world." Film images are seen overhead and on either side of the shuttle craft as well as up front. The six axis simulator in the domed theater "creates an incredibly realistic and convincing journey." Visitors, after the ride, disembark into a full scale reproduction of the Promenade from Star Trek: Deep Space Nine which houses assorted retail shops.

Other areas in Star Trek: The Experience include the History of the Future which is a museum-like exhibit that features authentic Star Trek costumes, weaponry, make-up, special effects, and props used in the series and in the eight motion pictures that were made. There is also a photo-morphing studio where guests can be photographed as their favorite character. In Quark's Restaurant & Bar visitors can enjoy exotic named drinks and foods—all based on the specific Star Trek "language" and "culture." The 22-minute experience is a rich and entertaining one. Costumed "characters" help to move the more than 2000 space travelers through the entire space in an hour. The experience includes one bridge, two loading docks, and two motion simulation rides. ■

HARRAH'S CASINO

Harrah's Hotel/Casino, Atlantic City, NJ

Interior Design
Daroff Designs, Inc., Philadelphia, PA

Principal in Charge
Karen Daroff

Director of Design
Martin Komitzky

Project Manager
Alina Jakubski

Project Architect
Gregg Olmstead

Senior Designer
Richard Marencic

Specifications
Susan Udovich

Signage
Glen Swantak/Simone Makoul

Architect
Bower, Lewis Thrower, Architects

Photography
Elliot Kaufman

Following the design concept of the previous renovations by Daroff Designs of Philadelphia, this new gaming area in the Casino is a further evolution of the original marine theme of the designers.

Throughout the design, there are undulating waves floating overhead and a liberal use of clear and blue glass. The "waves" continue to flow underfoot on the custom designed carpeting. Curved walls, wave-like, back-lit fascia panels along the perimeter walls, and the round columns topped with internally illuminated lotus-like glass caps all further the marine ambience at Harrah's, Atlantic City. Suspended between the blue suspended ceiling "waves" are glass bubbles, circles and "donuts" that sug-

gest air bubbles rising up through the water. Like the lobby, the fluid feeling of the design is enhanced by the blue, green and copper palette. The "High Roller" pits are accented with rich, red upholstered chairs and by the finish of the curvilinear, green topped, tables.

According to the designers, "It was management's desire to introduce the beauty and spirit of the site and its surrounding waterways into the hotel's interior." The overall objective was to create "an environment that translates the tranquility and beauty of the ocean through colors, lighting and finishes into the form and structure of the hotel." As these pictures show, the new design accomplished all it was meant to do. ■

CAESAR'S CASINO

Caesar's Hotel/Casino, Atlantic City, NJ

Design
**Brennan Beer Gorman Monk/Interiors,
New York, NY**

Architect
Cope Linder Assoc., Philadelphia, PA

Casino Design Consultant
Grana, Bonnett Assoc., P.C.

Lighting Designs
WGSS Lighting

Photography
Tom Crane

The new Caesar's Casino in Atlantic City through bold colors, shapes and forms, "takes guests on a journey through time to Ancient Rome." Guests enter the spectacular, six story casino/hotel where they are immediately enveloped in the tremendous feeling of space and the breathtaking view of the Coloseum's dramatically lit arches and statuary. The structural rhythm, played by repeating arches and towering Corinthian columns accented in gold, is set off by the bold colored, patterned carpeting of richly hued blue, red and gold. The casino is located at ground level below the Temple Lobby.

The casino is enriched with a 14 ft. coffered ceiling adorned with gilded ornamental moldings. The gaming areas are framed with fluted, stone Corinthian columns. Small statuary, set in decorative niches, are set above the slot machines and "the cool, stone wall surfaces—rich in ancient Roman imagery and architectural details"—provide a balance to the rich colors and fabrics used in the casino. Large pieces of "classic" statuary are highlighted throughout this space to reinforce the Roman theme. Cages areas are camouflaged with fluted stone pilasters, decorative pediments and stone and metal grillwork. ∎

HARRAH'S SMOKEY MOUNTAINS CASINO

Harrah's Hotel Casino, Cherokee, NC

Design
**Daroff Design, Inc.,
Philadelphia, PA**

Principal in charge
Karen Daroff

Principal/Project Manager
Norman Holloway, AIA

Project Architect
Gregg Olmstead, AIA

Senior Designer
Martin Komitzky

CADD
Roger Cecuna

Graphics/Signage
Glen Swantak/Simone Makoul

Architects of Record
Cunningham, Hamilton, Quiter

Principal in Charge
Tom Hoskens, AIA

Photography
Elliot Kaufman, N.Y.

The theme, devised by Daroff Design, for Harrah's Casino located in the Great Smokey Mountains—home of the Cherokee Indians—is based on lodge-style architecture, the colors and rich culture of the Cherokees and the logs and stones indigenous and thus readily available in this western part of North Carolina.

Guests, as they arrive, are treated to a state-of-the-art animatronics sound and light show which includes thunder and lightning. The interior space, with high bay areas, suggests the

limitless feeling of the great outdoors. The outdoor/rustic ambience is further enhanced by the wood columns with carvings of eagles and bears and the murals of the Smokey Mountains executed on cutout, back-lit panels. The strong colors carry through the "spirit and culture" of the Cherokee people.

The 50,000 sq. ft. casino is set in the center of the 170,000 sq. ft. space with a circulation path surrounding it. Patrons can follow the path to other attractions such as restaurants, the retail area and the child-friendly entertainment facility. Lighting effects simulate different times of the day—from sunrise to sunset—and into the evening sky filled with twinkling stars. The "outdoors" is brought indoors with the signage that represents rivers, mountains and trees along with the generous use of local timber and stone. ■

MOHEGAN SUN CASINO

**Mohegan Sun Casino Resort,
Mootville, CT**

Design
**Concept & Themed Interiors:
The Rockwell Group, New York, NY**

Architects
**Brennan Beer Gorman Architects,
New York, NY**

Photography
Paul Warchol

The Mohegan Sun Casino Resort is located on the 240-acre Mohegan Indian reservation overlooking the Thames River in Connecticut. It is the ancestral home of the Mohegan Tribe of North American Indians and one of the major design directives for the Rockwell Group of New York was to "embrace and highlight the Mohegan Indian culture" in the design. "Our design solution focuses on realizing and integrating the Mohegan mythology into the 600,000 sq. ft. project that consists of gaming, restaurant, entertainment and leisure spaces."

The Rockwell design is based on the lunar calendar (thirteen moon cycles). The gaming area is circular and represents the earth and it can be entered from each of its four cardinal points. These entrances represent the four seasons. The east entrance's stone fountain symbolically becomes the spring run-off of the melting snow. Winter is on the north and it is represented by a raised fire cauldron. Medallions, in the entrance floors, as well as the murals in the surround, show typical Mohegan activities during the various seasons.

Guests visually "step down" from the lofty entrances to the lower ceilinged portals onto the gaming floor. Above each entryway are can- tilevered panels decorated with fruits, flowers and designs appropriate to the particular season. The signs are held by wood frames. The seasonal theme continues to develop with real wood trees (where they can be touched) topped with branches. The extended trunks and branches are made of resin. The" leaves" on the trees indicate the seasons; white for winter; red and gold for autumn; bright green for summer. The carpets in each gaming area repeat the coloration and patterns of the "leaves."

At the very center of the circular casino is the 10,000 sq. ft. Wolf Bar. It was named in honor of the Mohegans who call themselves The Wolf People. ■

NY/NY CASINO

NY/NY Hotel Casino,
Las Vegas, NV

Interior Design
Yates-Silverman, Irvine, CA

Architect
Gaskin & Bezanski, Las Vegas, NV

Photography
Courtesy of NY/NY Hotel Casino

"The city that never sleeps"—a.k.a. New York City—has been brought to life in a slightly reduced scale and in a greatly enhanced version in the City of Lights—a.k.a. Las Vegas. NY/NY Hotel/Casino, a joint venture between MGM Grand and Primadonna Resorts, is located at the Tropicana and Las Vegas Blvd. intersection. In one third the actual size, the visual extravaganza features reproductions of the Statue of Liberty, the Chrysler Building, the Empire State Building, and other noted NYC landmarks. Encompassing all of these famous structures is a Coney Island style roller coaster.

"The uncanny realism of the NYC theme provides pizzazz, color and energy" to the 84,000 sq. ft. gaming casino inside the glittering and glowing "island" of buildings. The casino, in a space equal to two football fields, not only features the "action" craved by the gamesters but the setting also recalls the excitement and "danger" of the New York City ambience. "As casino patrons experience the pulse

of downtown Manhattan through a variety of sites and attractions, they also can enjoy gaming in one of the most state-of-the-art establishments in the U.S."

Surrounded by dimensionalized facades like the N.Y. Stock Exchange, Greenwich Village, a racetrack setting and even a flirtatious Statue of Liberty doing a "Marilyn Monroe" upswept skirt routine, gamblers can try their luck at any of the 71 tables of Blackjack, Craps, Roulette, Baccarat, Pai Gow, Pai Gow Poker and Keno as well as at any of the 2400 state-of-the-art slot machines.

For those who prefer professional sports and horse racing, there is a themed Race and Sports Book which was designed to resemble an historic race track. Here, guests are welcome to enjoy racing from around the country via telecast.

The downtown NYC urban look is enhanced throughout by the carpeted paths which are patterned to resemble city streets littered with theater stubs and gaming tickets. These paths direct the patrons to the smoking and non-smoking areas of the casino. ■

SPACEQUEST CASINO

Las Vegas Hilton, Las Vegas, NV

Conceptual and Interior Design
TSL, Los Angeles, CA

Planning & Art Direction
Richard Lewis, FISP

Design Team
Richard Lewis, J. Adams, J. Snyder, F. George

Production
G. Goldberg, T. Subagio

Executive Architect
**Cuningham Group/Solberg+Lowe,
Los Angeles, CA**

Show Producer
Metavision, Burbank, CA

Lighting
JK Design Group

Photography
Greg Cava

The Cuningham Group / Solberg+Lowe organization working with TSL created this 22,000 sq. ft. futuristic casino in the Las Vegas Hilton hotel. Every surface of the casino, which houses 400 slots and eight Black Jack tables, was carefully designed to "transport guests directly to the 24th century." Highlights in the design include three giant windows, 12 ft. x 25 ft. which "simulate the view of the orbiting Earth, while offering scenes of spacecrafts docking at SpaceQuest."

There is also a pulsating rocket booster, a docked flying saucer above the StarQuest bar, crackling bunched tubes of neon and space related mechanical apparatus bulging out from the wall surfaces. A glowing path of glass pavers, illuminated by a series of changing colored lights, runs the length of the casino. Bundles of fiber optic cables, on the walls and ceiling, create myriad lighting effects that add to the out-in-space experience. The fiber optic designs also twinkle like orbiting galaxies on the surface of the roulette tables. The SpaceQuest logo is "painted" with a rainbow of fiber optics piercing the black felt of the Black Jack tables.

SpaceQuest's designers used high tech materials, sophisticated audio effects and breathtaking visual technology to "establish an immersive and realistic space age environment." Stage and movie specialists worked closely with the architects/designers to create the sensational effects visible throughout the casino. The giant space windows, previously mentioned, are actually colossal rear projection theater screens and the images are coordinated on the three screens to produce the illusion that the casino and the patrons in it are all in orbit. Spaceship arrivals and departures are announced over the PA system to further the illusion.

SpaceQuest is only one part of a two part space extravaganza at the Las Vegas Hilton. The gaming casino is free for all to enter but beyond —at the end of the colorfully illuminated glass block path—is Star Trek: The Experience. Here an admission is charged for the entertainment/ motion simulation ride complex which is based on the TV series and the Hollywood films of Star Trek. The Star Trek: The Experience area, also shown in this book, is a joint venture of Paramount Parks Division of Viacom International and the Las Vegas Hilton. ■

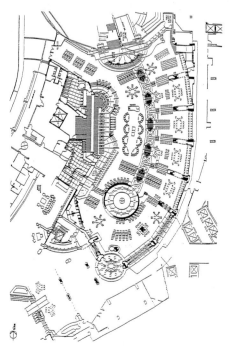

HARRAH'S HIGH LIMITS CASINO

Harrah's, Tahoe, NV

Design
Creative Resource Associates,
Culver City, CA

Photography
Robert Miller

A former 8500 sq. ft. coffee shop and Keno lounge in Harrah's Tahoe Hotel was converted into the exciting new High Limits Casino. The design directive to CRA—Creative Resource Associates of Culver City—was to "create a truly memorable experience"—especially for the "avid, experienced gambler." The result, illustrated here, bespeaks of the elegance of Lake Tahoe and the grandeur of the Sierra Nevada mountains. The lounge area, adjacent to the game tables and slots, not only relates to the gaming area but also conveys the ambience of "a private home on the banks of Lake Tahoe" in a "rustic, Alpine elegant style."

To open up the spatial volume of the new casino area, the floor was dropped 18 in., the existing ceiling was eliminated and the structural beams were relocated. Vaulted ceilings of tongue and groove Douglas pine with substantial truss framing members provide volume throughout the casino while heavy timbers, "peeler poles" and natural stone add a grand and solid texture to the space. The casino is furnished with large, comfortable pieces upholstered with rich fabrics as well as custom millwork, silk wall coverings and draperies with tie-backs. The color palette includes yellow gold on the walls over the limestone blocks, deep blue and burgundy fabrics and

mahogany laminate facings for the pit stations in the gaming area. All of this adds up to a "very residential feel" especially in the lounge area. Murals and silk Aspen trees also reaffirm the casino's background.

Large round iron and glass chandeliers, with decorative cutouts of deer and pine trees—to recall the locale—are used throughout for the ambient lighting. Added to these are the uplights on the ceiling beams and the wall sconces. According to Geoff Andres, director of Slot Operations at the hotel, "Uplighting not only works for a feeling of warmth, but is also conducive to slot players since the light does not reflect on the glass fronts of the slots." ■

STAR CITY GAMING CASINO

Star City, Sydney, Australia

Design
**The Hillier Group, Princeton, NJ
and Cox Richardson Architects &
Partners**

Project Directors
Hank Abernathy & John Richardson

Project Designer
Philip Cox

Project Architect
Jenny Watt

Technical Director
Peter Langley

Casino Project Architect
John Ilett

Casino Consultant
Michael A. Demling Assoc.

Theming Designer
Landmark Design Group

Photography
Patrick Bingham Hall

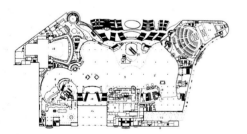

S tar City is a spectacular showplace that plays a major role in the revitalization of Sydney's historic Pyrmont Harbour. The over two million sq. ft. entertainment complex includes the 156,000 sq. ft. casino, shown here, as well as a private gaming hall of 19,000 sq. ft. Among the other facilities included in the giant complex are seven restaurants, seven specialty bars, retail shopping, meeting and function halls that can accommodate up to 1,000 guests, a 350-room hotel and the Lyric theatre which is also shown in this book.

Patrons can enter the Casino through either of two spectacular entrances. From the porte cochere entry they can glide up the escalator through "dueling jets of fire and water" or they can take a "safer" route that takes them through the underground rail station entry. Here they have only to pass under a waterfall that cascades down from 60 ft. overhead.

The gaming area itself consists of 1500 slot machines and 160 tables. Given the waterside location, the designers have used water as the primary decorative motif throughout. There are four zones here and each is themed differently. The Sports Betting area has a ceiling filled with bright colored silk ribbon-like streamers that look like colorful sails or the silks of horse-racing. Murals, on the walls, are filled with athletic sports activities. The other three areas take their inspiration from the Australian landscape: the desert outback—rich in desert ochers and golds; the Australian sky of dark blue studded with myriad stars; and the underwater theme based on the Great Barrier Reef. This area sparkles with vivid greens and yellows. Thousands of glass bubbles descend from the deep blue washed ceiling along with algae-like ribbons. The transparent cylindrical aquariums that are on view as guests descend to the casino prepare them for this underwater realm. A Moroccan motif was used for the "high rollers" special gaming area and the special elevators for these patrons are also themed: The English Club Room; the Oriental Room; and the Taj Mahal Room. ■

EMPERYAL CASINO

Penta Hotel, Istanbul, Turkey

Design
**DiLeonardo International, Inc.
Warwick, RI**

Photography
Yavna Onar

Adjacent to the five star Penta Hotel in Istanbul is the new Emperyal Casino, a 12,000 square meter space. The casino was designed as three inter-related areas. One is the slot machine zone with a service bar and a sunken area for novelty gaming. There is also a double height game table zone with its own raised bar and lounge and a buffet style restaurant. For the "high rollers," the V.I.P. private gaming area and mezzanine lounge has its own special entrance.

The designers, DiLeonardo International of Warwick, RI have kept the overall atmosphere light and airy. A relaxed, resort-like atmosphere is achieved by combining the light color palette with the spectacular view of the Marmara Sea as seen through the panoramic windows. "Clean and fresh" hues of melon, amber pink, lavender and pale blues predominate in the carpets, fabrics, tiles and marbles. Moresque patterned Italian glass mosaics are applied to the walls in the circulation areas and the grand staircase. To reinforce the open and airy feeling, many plants are used throughout—some in wall mounted planters veneered with jewel-toned tiles. Also, a large carved and etched glass skylight crowns the double height gaming area. Peach colored neon cove lighting "dances on the reflective ceiling of the gaming area to reinforce the upscale and sophisticated look of the Emperyal Casino." ■

CASINO ROYALE

**Grandeur of the Seas
Cruise Ship**

Design
**Howard Snoweiss Design Group,
Coral Gables, FL**

Shipyard
**Kvaerner Masa-Yards,
Helsinki**

Snoweiss Project Team
Diane Stratton/Keith Briggs

Photography
**Nancy Robinson Watson,
Castine, ME**

The small but dynamic Casino Royale on the Grandeur of the Seas cruise ship pays tribute to Las Vegas and in the limited space attempts to capture and generate the excitement, razzle dazzle and fun experience one associates with Las Vegas casinos, the themed hotels and the kinetic night-time lighting.

The area is predominantly a color scheme of red and blue. With each color intensifying the other and both creating a feeling of festivity, the excitement begins with the illuminated glass columns with flaring capitals and the gilded lion—a tribute to the MGM lion that is one of the attractions on Las Vegas Blvd. Blue carpets are bordered in red and the stools in front of the slots are upholstered in red. Friezes of neon and mirror, over the slots, add to the sizzle and Las Vegas quality of the space. One of the fun focal areas in the casino is the glass floor under which is revealed a cache of coins, jewels, trinkets and

treasure—all illuminated. The gamesters can walk over all this treasure. The designers took advantage of the recess in the deck to create this stepper-stopper.

In addition to the MGM lion, the fiber optic lighting, art glass and neon, there are many sculptural illusions to recognizable Vegas themed landmarks integrated into the design. ■

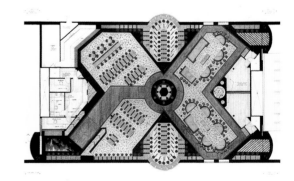

CASINO ROYALE

Rhapsody of the Seas
Cruise Ship

Design
**Howard Snoweiss Design Group,
Coral Gables, FL**

Shipyard
Chantiers de L' Atlantiqua

Snoweiss Project Team
Daine Stratton/Keith Briggs

Photography
Nancy Robinson Watson, Castine, ME

lights. "Its sparkling, jewel-like surfaces feature murals with classical motifs and twinkling stars that depict the 12 astrological constellations." Added to this are the illuminated "mega worlds" created by glass artist, Josh Simpson, as well as neon lit glass clouds, sun shaped chandeliers and mosaic floor patterns with astrological motifs. For extra emphasis, Lady Luck appears in "cosmos styled," life-size sculptures.

Included in this ocean going casino are almost 200 gaming stations which include five Black Jack, two Caribbean Poker, roulette and Craps tables and about 150 slot and slant top machines.

A separate bar can seat 17 and it is equipped with five TV monitors for viewing sports events. In addition to all this, the designers have overlaid the design with dynamic, Las Vegas-style lighting effects. ■

T he casino aboard the Royal Caribbean line's Rhapsody of the Seas was intended to be a "tribute to the cosmos." Passengers enter the casino by passing by the "window to the Universe"—a kinetic, 3D experience featuring art glass, fiber optic lighting and out-of-this-world sound effects. Focal to the design of this area is the enormous dome in the center of the casino which consists of concentric layers of circular ceiling forms outlined in colored neon and bands of tracer

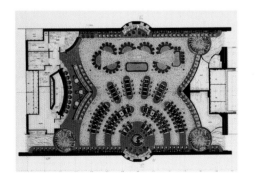

THAT'S ENTERTAINMENT THEATER

Legend of the Seas Cruise Ship

Design
**Howard Snoweiss Design Group,
Coral Gables, FL**

Shipyard
Chantiers de L'Atlantique

Snoweiss Project Team
Kelly Gonzalez/Peter Beggs

Photography
Nancy Robinson Watson

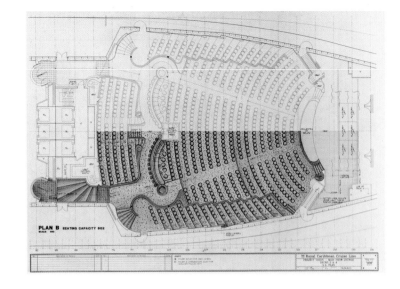

This design, the That's Entertainment Theater on the Royal Caribbean International's Legend of the Seas, was the continuation of the on-going design partnership between the cruise line and Howard Snoweiss Design firm of Coral Gables, FL.

The two level theater is entered through paired passageways whose ornate nine foot plus panels are embellished with filigree, crystals, and stars. These partially glass panels are back lit and they were developed by Tom Graboski Assoc. following an original Snoweiss design.

Instead of an overhanging balcony, there are a series of stepped terraces—one on either side and a third in the rear. They have relatively low elevations of about three feet off the deck, and the glass, edge-lit, railings twinkle with etched stars There are dome-like chandeliers above each interior entryway and a much larger version is mounted in the center of the theater. They are made up of hundreds of Treidri crystals imported from Austria and assembled in Norway. The entire theater of almost 14,000 sq. ft. has only four perceptible supporting pillars where there usually are as many as 16. This is a boon to spectators who are all consequently gifted with unobstructed sight lines.

The color palette combines amethyst, gold, and sapphire blues—"all rich, resplendent colorations." A gold toned marble veined in violet and inlaid with bronze stars, á la Hollywood

Blvd., is complemented by a custom Axminster wool rug that features multicolored ribbons, stars and stellate objects on a neutral ground. Amethystine- stained birds eye maple veneer panels flank the proscenium stage which can be extended or elevated via a pneumatic lift. The stage draperies are embroidered tapestries by Wendy Dolan. The curtain, 38 ft. wide by 16 ft. high, is a colorful amalgam of Austrian crystals, sequins, beads, lurex and lame.

The side walls of the auditorium contain woven threads of gold and a complementary series of corrugated, floor-to-ceiling, panels which are accented with cast brass stars. The panels are inlaid with purple stained wood and light strips. Each wall, port and starboard, also features a lustrous, concave, back-lit panel 12 ft. wide by nine ft. high. They are composed of assorted glass fragments, cut, layered and fired by Karen Sepanski of Detroit. Throughout the theater commissioned artworks have been incorporated into the lavish design to create this scintillating space. ■

BROADWAY MELODIES THEATER

**Rhapsody of the Seas
Cruise Ship**

Design
**Howard Snoweiss Design Group,
Coral Gables, FL**

Shipyard
Chantiers de L'Atlantique

Snoweiss Project Team
**Jim O'Shaughnessy/Jodi Barozinsky
Peter Beggs**

Photography
Nancy Robinson Watson

The 867 seat Broadway Melodies Theater is a floating entertainment center. It sits on the Royal Caribbean cruise ship, Rhapsody of the Seas—a 2435 passenger vessel.

According to the interior designer, Howard Snoweiss, who has designed several floating theaters, "There isn't one bit of space that isn't customized" in the theater. Yet the auditorium has wide aisles, generous leg space between the rows and even illuminated drink holders on each seat so that drinks don't tipple over when the sea gets choppy. The Broadway Melodies theme is set in the two entrance vestibules where the carpeting features an undulating piano keyboard set within a border of musical notes. The keyboard motif is repeated inside the art deco inspired auditorium in a series of illuminated, wall mounted sculptured glass panels. The two level theater has upholstered seats, carpeted floors and special acoustical wall panels that all work with the metal ceiling to get the desired effect from the installed audio and acoustical systems. Figured wood paneling,

columns sheathed in brass and brass railings all add a "nautical" quality to the green and gold color scheme. The damask-like upholstery emphasizes the gold color which blends with the green of the figured carpeting.

A focal point in the design is the unusual lighting fixture over the orchestra seats. In design, it reiterates the undulating piano keyboard introduced out front. As the house lights dim, the eight glass panels gently rise and dip to affect a rippling, wave-like effect and then the lights within slowly diminish—and the show goes on! ∎

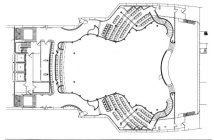

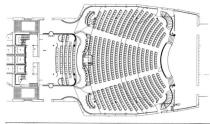

PALLADIUM THEATER

Grandeur of the Seas
Cruise Ship

Design
Howard Snoweiss Design, Coral Gables, FL

Shipyard
Kvaerner Masa-Yards, Helsinki

Snoweiss Project Team
**Kelly Gonzalez/Peter Beggs
Jodi Barozinsky/Philip Martin
Marlyns Ronquillo**

Photography
Nancy Robinson Watson

The challenge was to create a two level, Broadway-style theater on a cruise ship where the designer is restricted by the deck to deck heights, the lengths and widths. The designer, Howard Snoweiss, had to create space for the 870 custom, continental-style seats with maximized viewing in the constrained space while still accommodating the ADA standards of 1:12 ramping throughout.

A formidable entrance to the theater was erected which somehow minimized the long walkway into the auditorium caused by the fire stairs and the placement of technical equipment. A vestibule area was affected by the use of inlaid marble floors and the foreshortened entry is enhanced by the highly focal, back-lit, Lalique style glass panels and marble flooring. Custom wall sconces and fixtures dramatically illuminate the entry. By cutting back the balcony seating area to a sweeping curve, the viewer's sense of entry into the theater is focused on the custom stage curtain.

Internally lit alabaster urns frame the paired staircases inside and twin, two story high illuminated glass towers flank the thrust proscenium. The elaborate curtain is made up of layers of iridescent fabrics overlaid with multiple images of celebrated entertainers. The softly curved soffit above, like a curved chandelier, is composed of thousands of crystals. To incorporate the desired theatrical lighting, lights are set

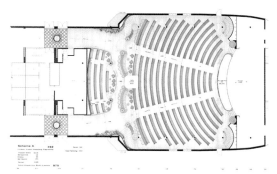

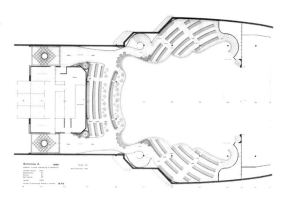

into the sides of the stage behind custom glass panels. Special sculptural coves, in the ceiling, conceal the "follow" spots and other lamps. Other technical equipment includes an overhead video screen projection system, computerized winches and an orchestra pit that goes up and down. Full scale musicals can be mounted here.

The auditorium has "voluminous ceilings", inlaid marble floors and walls of birds eye maple as well as padded acoustical panels. "To give this space a unique identity and sense of elegance unique to cruise ship environment, many custom art pieces as well as architectural details were incorporated into the design of the space." Technically, every seat is a great seat in the Palladium. ∎

BILOXI GRAND THEATRE

Biloxi, MS

Design
Cuningham Group, Minneapolis, MN

Principal in Charge
John Cuningham, FAIA

Project Manager
Mark Sopko, AIA

Team Leader
Wade Morgan

Interior Design
**Susan Jacobson/Cheryl Winger/
Michael Dant/Margaret Clark**

Photography
Christian M. Korab

A n exciting and entertaining part of
the Grand Casino Biloxi Resort is the
Biloxi Grand Theatre designed by the
Cuningham Group of Minneapolis. It is
the home to a Las Vegas style theatrical
production and it is also used for special events
like headline entertainers, concerts, local civic
activities, conventions and festivals.

The three story, almost all glass facade is gently curved and recommends the fun inside through the creative mix of color and light that is evident through the transparent face. The exterior curve is echoed in the radial arced patterns that appear in the carpet design and in the curved glass wall showcases. The interior is illuminated by opulent chandeliers composed of thousands of hand blown crystal tear drops. The chandeliers and the pilasters also recall the sinuous curve motif. The custom carpeting, mentioned above, was designed by the Cuningham Group for this specific use and it is further animated with colorful stars, planets and comets. This adds a "sense of merriment" to the Theatre's more dramatic public spaces. ■

LYRIC THEATRE

Star City, Sydney, Australia

Design
The Hillier Group & Cox Richardson Architects & Partrners

Design Team
Hank Abernathy/John Richardson/Philip Cox/Jenny Watt/Peter Longley/Mac Rawley/Tim Folland/Lee Cogle/Tim Jeffrey/Steve Hubbard/Daniel McCahon/Susan Hodges/Julia Beckingate/Peyton Riley/Bruce Lincoln/Paul Hemmings/David Radford

Photography
Patrick Bingham-Hall

The 2000-seat Lyric Theatre is an important part of the new Star City project. The Star City project, which also appears in this book, is a 2.2 million sq. ft. casino complex which in addition to gaming facilities includes a multi-use entertainment complex which attracts more than 20,000 visitors a day.

The Lyric Theatre is a state-of-the-art auditorium for opera, ballet and musical comedy performances. The three tier, horseshoe seating design "provides every patron with an intimate relationship with stage and performers alike," The seats are arranged in continental style rows with 1000 seats in the stalls (orchestra) and 500 in each of the two circles (balconies). The sides of the circles extend around the auditorium and engage the proscenium frame to "establish a strong connection between the audience seating area and the performance space." According to the design firms, Cox Richardson Architects and The Hillier Group, "The objective of the design was to produce an acoustically warm and intimate, visually rich and exciting space for the production and enjoyment of musical theatre."

Warm colors, native Australian woods (deep red eucalyptus veneers) indigo carpets,upholstery and trim and carefully organized geometric patterns—like the acoustic textured walls of the hall—create a visually and acoustically soothing environment. Seating for patrons with physical disabilities and hearing impairments is dispersed throughout the general seating areas. The auditorium is capped by a 50 ft by 75 ft elliptical mural by Colin Lancey.

The abstract painting represents musicians being led by a conductor.

Each tier of seating is served by its own gracious lobby and they all have awesome views of the Sydney skyline. The lobbies are connected by a sculptural staircase that features glass treads and landings. The glass stair and the theatre bars are all housed in a spectacular four story glass drum that is supported by an intricate web of steel cables. The building, itself, literally floats on huge neoprene pads. They were designed to prevent the transmission of noise from the outside including the commuter rail line that runs directly below the theatre.

The orchestra pit can accommodate a full orchestra and it can be raised to stage level and even used as a thrust stage. A sculptural fly tower houses a 75, single purchase flying system capable of lifting 50 tons of scenery or performance related material. ■

ORCHESTRA HALL

Symphony Center, Chicago, IL

Design
Skidmore Owings & Merrill, Chicago, IL

Photography
Hedrich Blessing, Chicago, IL

The classic Symphony Center on S. Michigan Ave in Chicago was originally opened in 1904 and was designed by the famous architect of that day, Daniel Burnham. The Georgian style building houses Orchestra Hall. A year or so ago the newly expanded and renovated Chicago Symphony Orchestra's home was reopened as restored by the Chicago architectural firm of Skidmore Owings & Merrill. The architects, through significant teamwork and planning efforts, developed a design "that would overlay the historic hall with state-of-the-art technology, creating a venue that would be competitive through the 21st century."

The new complex includes renovated public and performance spaces in the existing structure. To improve the acoustics in the hall there was a massive "increase in volume in the main hall, the stage reconfiguration and the addition of a system of adjustable acoustical elements that are hidden from view." In addition, a new steel and glass acoustical canopy was installed to reflect sound across the stage and into the audience.

The audience chamber has a seating capacity of 2600. It was reconfigured to increase seat size and row depth for the patron's comfort. S.O.M.'s project manager, Brian Jack, said, "We lost a couple of hundred seats when we brought in the side wall. We added seating behind the stage which was a logical solution to a practical problem." The terraced seating, behind the orchestra, is a familiar concept in Europe but new to the U.S. The architects reused the original ornamental plaster details within the hall so that, though reshaped, it retains the essence of Burnham's original grand scheme.

A public arcade, just north of the main hall, connects the Michigan Ave. entrance to a multi-storied rotunda which becomes the new focus of the expanded complex. The rotunda includes more and improved circulation space, public

amenities, and larger lobby spaces. The artistic support wing, connected to the rotunda, provides the orchestra with much needed back up space; a large rehearsal hall, which also doubles as a function room, additional dressing areas for visiting orchestras and a mechanical plant for the complex.

According to Daniel Barenboim, the music director of the CSO, by transforming the 25,000 sq. ft. orchestra hall into the 65,000 sq. ft. Symphony Center, "a true festival hall" has been created that will draw more people into Chicago's cultural life and establish the city as a "world class arts center." ∎

A.C.T.
A CONTEMPORARY
THEATER

Seattle, WA

Design
Callison Architecture, Seattle, WA

Project Manager
George Wickwire

Project Architect
Gil Jaffee

Project Designer
Gary Wakatsuki

Photography
Steve Keating

The former historic Eagles Auditorium, in Seattle, was renovated by the Callison Architecture firm, of the same city, to accommodate A Contemporary Theater's new facilities as well as 44 low income housing units on the building's top four floors. The project involved restoring the existing seven story Eagles Temple Building to accommodate three performing arts auditoria. The architects had to also provide, in addition to work shops and administrative offices, opportunities for daily interaction between staff and actors—and make use of maximum daylight.

The interior and exterior were restored to "their original grandeur" with new exterior terra cotta finishes and new interior decorative plasterwork. The Callison team had to orchestrate a large number of often conflicting interests among which was reconciling a painstaking restoration process with the highly technical requirements of the various performance spaces. Of paramount importance was "retaining the actor-audience intimacy" for which A.C.T. is known. One theater called for a thrust stage with features tailored to A.C.T.'s character and purpose. Another one is a very intimate space—a theater in the round—and the last functions as a flexible, cabaret-style auditorium. Only one large space existed and

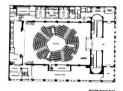

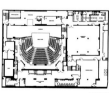

that was too large for the thrust stage. Where walls and floors had to be moved, the new stairs and support areas were designed as not to be perceived as different from the original ones. In the arena theater, the technical lighting and sound equipment was suspended in the space and "touches the original fabric as lightly as possible".

In the support and lobby spaces, Callison followed A.C.T.'s artistic director's vision. Some of the areas were decorated by A.C.T.'s set designer as integral to the idea that the whole

space is part of the "total experience" and yet each space is distinctly different in character from the next.

This is a place where people gather to share an entertainment experience. Between 300 and 1000 patrons attend A.C.T. performances six nights a week in this landmark building which is playing a vital part in downtown Seattle's revitalization. The A.C.T. project won the Urban Land Institute's award for Rehabilitation projects as well as an AIA merit award. ■

RED'S REC ROOM

Edmonton, AB, Canada

Design
JPRA Architects, Farmington Hills, MI

President
James P. Ryan, AIA

Principal in Charge
David Peterhans/Ron Rea

Project Manager
Matt Woods

Sr. Designer
Ellen Devine

Graphic Design
Ron Rue

Photography
Merle Prosky, Edmonton

The Edmonton Mall in Edmonton is the world's largest mall and occupying 100,000 sq. ft. the mammoth space is the giant prototype for Red's Rec Room. Designed by JPRA Architects of Farmington Hills, MI, Red's includes a 250-seat restaurant, a 350-seat club/theater as well as fun activities like bowling, billiards, game areas and even a brew pub.

The design objectives for creating this walk-around experience included; "make guests move through with gusto"; create a traffic flow with maximum access and excitement; and bring together diverse elements into a cohesive whole so that every zone is enticing and inviting. The designers converted the former, two-level IKEA furniture store into this tongue-in-cheek recreation of mid-America's recreation room of the 1950s and 1960s. Red's recalls the days of wood paneled basements, hi-fidelity stereos, Twister (TM) and Lava Lamps. In some areas, genuine vintage Laz-E-Boy recliners are offered to patrons who really want to lie back and relax—and get into the Rec Room mood..

The designers created a huge opening between the two levels, enhanced by a catwalk, that allows guests to view many spaces in all the assorted zones. "Eye contact above, below, and around the space is a key element" in the design. A disk jockey's platform, above the main bar, overlooks the vast dance floor. An 18

ft. rotating bowling trophy brings the D.J.'s area into focal prominence. Real stadium seating is adjacent to the stage. Red's Rec Room becomes all: playroom, party room, TV room, and "the coolest place in the house."

JPRA accomplished this with colors, materials and the arts and artifacts of the period. The exuberant strong colors and the "over the top" decor, based on 1950s and 1960's models, "embody everyone's idea of bad taste rec rooms celebrated in modern form." As one might expect—with a name like "Red's"—red in all its many incarnations is the major color in the bold palette. Instead of a black ceiling in the night club, it has been painted purple—"to bring more energy to the space."

In the dining area, patterned tiles—inspired by the '50s—is used while red and green plaid carpeting covers areas of both levels. In other zones, a black and green checkered carpet is laid "to carry on the spirit if not the letter of vintage linoleum." All around, knotty pine paneling, rafters and exposed piping continue the basement theme. Vintage floor lamps and

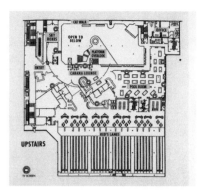

bric-a-brac are also incorporated into the overall design.

"More vintage pieces blend with contemporary interpretations of the same theme."

Since everything in Red's is bigger and better, there is an 11 by 15 ft. video screen set into the behemoth TV set and it is used for live broadcasts of the house band (Red's Rebels). A colossal, 20 ft. moose head flaunts 25 ft. neon antlers. A 12 ft. diameter bowling ball is set on a wall along with a sequenced collection of neon bowling pins. An 18 ft. foot

rainbow trout chases a neon lure through neon rippling water.

The bowling and games areas are designed to appeal to all ages. A futuristic bowling sensation, Cosmic Bowling, features glow-in-the-dark lanes, pins, and balls along with a Cosmic light show, lasers, fog effects and 25,000 watts of classic rock'n'roll." In addition, there is a Red's Attic, a retail area filled with quirky, campy collectibles such as Lava Lamps, Barbie Doll key-chains—and, of course, Red's logo branded merchandise. This is truly a "family entertainment center" on a giant scale. ∎

ENTROS

San Francisco, CA/Seattle, WA

Design
Entros Inc + NBBJ, Seattle, WA

Photography
Spike Nafford Photography, Seattle

I t started in Seattle and it is spreading. Entros newest venue is in San Francisco, but it continues the food/fun and games that started it all. The proprietors' original concept mixed good and fanciful foods with original, interactive games that were originated by Andy Forrest and Steve Brown. Stephen Brown says that they wanted to create

a setting where the so-called "isolating" effects of this age of technology could be counteracted by people reacting and interfacing with other people. It is like "Charades" and "Scavenger Hunt" brought up into the 21st century. Patrons are invited to participate in team activities—like a Scavenger Hunt with clues provided on touch screen computer stations. "Interface" is the millennium's answer to "Blind Man's Bluff" where the blindfolded partner wears a video camera headset that transmits what he would be seeing to his partner via closed circuit TV. The "seeing" partner then must guide the blindfolded one by voice through a series of experiences. Entros is providing a venue where people meet people, interact with people, have fun being with people and can also enjoy communal dining and drinking. It is "a social entertainment company." "We build mind and body games that bring people together," says Andy Forrest.

Within this "Intelligent Amusement Park," there are 25 different, interactive game activities. All are based on four structures: big toys, video games, multimedia odysseys, and electronic game shows. "Our games are based more on human touch. I like to think they (the games) are the human antidote for a technical

world." "Social interaction" is at the core of each game.

At the center of the 15,000 sq. ft. indoor "amusement park" is a bar and restaurant in what looks like a warehouse. Bright colors, shiny high-tech materials, festoons of lights, illuminated colored panels and theatrical lighting fixtures all add sparkle, fun and excitement to this focal area. The "rooms" surrounding this area have licensed or experimental games open to the patrons.

Entros has created an entertainment complex that appeals to both sexes. "It's hard for adults to find a place like this—to play like a kid in a social setting that's competitive mentally." "Unlike sports, we can't get rained out and anybody can play." ■

DAVE & BUSTERS

Toronto, ON, Canada

Design
Melvin Fain & Associates

Photography
Courtesy of Dave & Buster's

The Dave & Buster's phenomenon has spread across the country and even made it to England. The concept first evolved in a converted warehouse in Dallas. A few years later, after proving to be successful, a second venue was established at a shopping center in the Dallas area. There was no stopping this concept that combines "great food and great fun." Not only can one dine on really good food but added to the mix is a Viewpoint Bar—a pub-like setting with a 20-screen video dome where patrons can follow the of-the-moment sporting events or the guest can visit the D & B Showroom, a special events theater. In addition, there are assorted fun activities available from pocket billiards and shuffle board to virtual reality experiences and other electronic games in the game arcade.

In 1993, one year after D & B opened in Atlanta, that venue had already welcomed over one million guests. The Dave & Buster's flagship—a 70,000 sq. ft. space on Philadelphia's historic Delaware waterfront—became the most ambitious location to date when it opened in 1994. 1995 and 1996 saw openings in Chicago and 1996 was a big year with other openings in Bethesda, MD (outside of Washington, DC), and Hollywood, FL. The chain has now expanded to the west coast with operations in Ontario Mills, the Irvine Spectrum and Denver. The success of the operation is its appeal to so many. It is a fun place for dating, a great place to hang out and a most satisfactory family experience destination. There is something for everyone on the big but moderately priced menu and the dozens of entertainment opportunities available in the various play rooms. ■

KRAMER & EUGENE'S

Concord, NC

Architect/Designer
Aumiller Youngquist PC, Mt. Prospect, IL

Principal in Charge
Dave Kasprak

Project Manager
Laura Stoops

Photography
**Mark Ballogg, Steinkamp Ballogg,
Chicago, IL**

The 50,000 sq. ft. entertainment complex, Kramer & Eugene's, is located in Concord, NC. The facility includes an upscale billiards club, a 200-seat restaurant and an 80-seat lounge, a private business club with a lounge and library as well as a full banqueting facility.

The club was designed to look like a converted warehouse. A funky glass and stained wood, curved desk—near the entrance—serves as a control counter for the staff. Here there is a selection of cigars, K & E merchandise and ball sets to be used for pool rentals. K & E logo merchandise is also available in the retail space just beyond and here the rich copper slat wall and dark cherrywood become attractive backgrounds for the T-shirts, mugs and caps. The Sports Bar, straight ahead, is defined by a lively patterned copper soffit and purple and green wood patterned walls. There are built-in purple cushioned benches surrounding the bar and they serve to accommodate guests waiting to be seated. Surrounding the bar is a rail made up of pool balls—drilled and strung. On the inside of the rail there is seating for groups in fabric backed booths and banquettes. Loose tables complete the seating here. The curved bar has mother of pearl inlay trim and pool pockets (corner and side) like those on the actual pool table that are visible just beyond. The dome ceiling, over the bar, takes on the shape and

appearance of the #9 ball with a yellow stripe. Wood flooring with purple cherry wood pattern radiating out from the curved bar and the cove lighting and the halogen cable lights all add to the dramas and sparkle of this area.

Next to the bar is the warm and friendly restaurant finished in muted tones, mahogany stained wood and a bronze and gold mosaic tile brick oven. The focal points in the restaurant are the 16 ft. custom lighting fixtures made of brushed stainless steel, copper, frosted glass and with perforated metal accents. The public pool room boasts 20 rosewood and c opper, pocket Brunswick Gold Crown IV tables. The purple and green carpet provides an amusing pattern of cue sticks and the green lamp shades, over the tables, provide illumination for the games as well as for ambience. The cue racks are constructed of corrugated metal, back-lit, trimmed with perforated copper and stained cherry wood. The light green walls provide a quiet background for the pool-related artwork and framed memorabilia. For seating there are large wood spectator chairs with cut-out cue rests and arm and foot rests. For those who prefer to snack as they play, the high top eating counters are designed with green tinged galvanized aluminum tops and cherry wood edges.

To get to the second level there is a grand spiral staircase by the front entrance or guests can use the elevator. The free-standing, spiral staircase is enclosed within a glass tower that is anchored to the building. Dark gray porcelain tile treads radiate from the center and an open stainless steel and black accented hand rail provide support. The passenger elevator "provides a transition between the copper and stainless steel of the first floor with the elegant bronze accents on the second."

The second level focuses on the "Nine of Clubs," an area open only to business club members. It is elegantly designed and furnished with rich materials and unique fixtures. The palette here is hunter green, burgundy, plaids and warm leathers. There are several antique pool tables here amid the overstuffed, comfortable lounge chairs. Private business meetings can be held in the conference room. The Copperfield Room is a 3500 sq. ft. banquet facility and here the lighted cove ceiling, crown moldings and elegant wall coverings add luster to any special occasion.

Kramer & Eugene's has proven to be very successful and is a popular, up-scale entertainment venue in Concord. ∎

THE SUNSET CLUB

Charlotte, NC

Design
Shook Design Group, Charlotte, NC

Photography
Tim Buchman, Photography

The Sunset Club brings back an idea from another time in a smart new concept. This is a private venture "social club" that is positioned as a place to go before dinner, after theater or for late-night socializing. Located in an historic district that is fast becoming the city's "hottest entertainment and boutique shopping destination," the 3500 sq. ft. space combines drinking, smoking and meeting people in a most gracious manner.

The concept takes its name from a 1920s club, in Charlotte, that was founded by a group of industry leaders and financiers. As designed by Shook Design Group, it "evokes the elegance of the Cocktail era." The space features 14 ft. high ceilings, exposed brick walls and a "great room" as well as a raised seating area which is served by a double sided fireplace. There is a cocktail bar and a library alcove as well as a 200 box, custom designed humidor. The space is divided into eclectic groupings of big, leather covered lounge chairs and plushy sofas all romantically lit by shaded lamps. The palette is neutral with warm and earthy beiges, golds, light browns, terra cottas and deep red accents. Framed pictures, paintings and period artifacts add to the inviting ambience. The club can accommodate 100 guests with another 20 made welcome on the adjacent exterior patio.

This is a "members only" club and that makes it even more a place to be and be seen. It is "entertainment" for the special few. ■

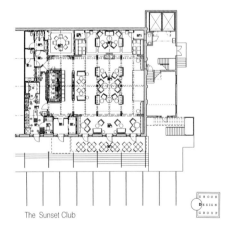

The Sunset Club

THE SCREENING
ROOM

Varick & Canal Sts., New York, NY

Design
Bogdanow Partners, Architects, New York, NY

Design Team
**Larry Bogdanow/Tom Schweitzer/
Christina Ziegler**

Photography
Robert Blosser/Eric Rank/Mihn & Wass

The Screening Room is a restaurant and movie theater. It was conceived and designed as a "cool place" for people in the film industry to hang out and to see films. The 6500 sq. ft. space combines a main theater space which can accommodate 130 patrons, a bar that can seat 15 and a dining room for 140 diners. There is also as mezzanine lounge, and two "I" rooms which are smaller film-viewing rooms.

The design concept by Bogdanow Partners Architects of New York is "current, stylish, up-to-date" but also is slightly retro to recapture some of the glamour of Hollywood in the 1930s, 1940s and 1950s. The result is a blend of new and old. There is a curved aluminum soffit over the lobby door, a polished mahogany bar, and up-to-the-minute technology for the film projection equipment. The "old" is present in the lounge furniture purchased from dealers, the reupholstered furniture, swag draperies hanging between the dining and bar areas and a large electric sign salvaged from an old sign shop which proclaims "Liquors" over the bar.

The designers specified a special carpet for the screening room and mezzanine and it is patterned in burgundy, gold, blue and fern green. This coordinates with the fabric on the seats in the theater and also the upholstery fabric used in the lounge. The ribbon pattern is meant to recall "ribbons" of celluloid film. The exposed brick walls complement the fabrics and the custom light fixtures along the theater walls are "unexpectedly dramatic and industrial."

A cafe and box office, on the south corner also serve as a waiting room and provide a look out on the action in Tribeca—where this new concept is located. ■

INDIAN MOTORCYCLE

Toronto, ON, Canada

Design
ll X lV Design Associates, Toronto, ON

Photography
David Whittaker, Toronto, ON

The Indian Motorcycle was first manufactured in 1901 but production ceased in 1953. In an effort to revitalize that brand name by a Canadian company, this project came into being. The owners refer to this combined cafe, bar, lounge, billiards parlour, entertainment space and boutique as a "brand shrine" but what it truly is is a fun, entertainment, dining space that respects the vintage quality of the product and the site.

Located in a landmark building in downtown, west end Toronto, the architects had to obtain approval for a new entrance into the building. To conceal the drab vistas around it, windows on the south and west sides were blocked off with shutters and cabinetry. Motorcycles can be moved in and out by means of the old freight elevator. The patron enters through double doors from the new corner entry lobby into a small, carefully merchandised boutique. The guest then passes between man-

nequins and under simple, steel pinned signage. The fixturing system, in the boutique, consists of maple horizontals framed in black stained wood with small metal logo plates applied. Cream walls, light maple flooring and satin nickel metal finishes provide a cool, crisp back drop for the products and the trademark Indian Motorcycle elements such as the motorcycle headlights and the skirted fender shapes. A complete motor cycle bay, in the window, is fitted with new and vintage bikes. The stone topped cash desk is clad in stainless steel. Also, located off the entry lobby, is the Cafe and Lounge.

Motorcycles appear throughout the space along with other memorabilia such as photos and bike artifacts many of which are housed in maple cases. As part of the "branding" approach to interior design, many materials and details refer back to the classic vehicle like the rubber foot rests used on the bar and drink rails, and the fender-like shape of the lounge chair arms. Actual bike lights are used to illuminate the stairs.

Existing natural maple floors were patched and repaired and, where necessary, matching flooring was installed. Columns and beams were painted dark charcoal and the drywall and wood ceiling were washed in soft cream tones. Stainless steel and polished chrome details contrast with the satin black, polyester resin finished table tops.

A new opening between the floors accommodates an elegant, open stair with solid maple treads, stainless steel handrail and a glass and steel balustrade. This becomes "a floating, transparent connection between the cafe and the upper level lounge." In the multipurpose area, a stage is provided for live performances, fashion shows and product launches. Bright red topped billiard tables are centered on the windows.

Cabinets and long niches above the drink rail display memorabilia. Area rugs define seating clusters of black leather sofas and honey chenille clad lounge chairs. These surround a focal and dramatic suspended fireplace.

The 50 ft. bar features an array of chrome draft towers and behind it are transparency boxes and video monitors which not only display historic visuals but promotional tie-ins with the bike and the company's other branded merchandise. ∎

CHELSEA PIERS SPORTS & ENTERTAINMENT COMPLEX

Pier 62, New York, NY

Architect
James G. Rogers lll, FAIA with Butler, Roger Baskett, New York, NY

Photography
Fred George. Courtesy of Chelsea Piers

Located between 17th and 23rd Streets along Manhattan's Hudson River is the 30 acre waterfront Sports Village and Entertainment Complex: Chelsea Piers. Four, long neglected but historic piers were transformed for over $100 million into the complex which includes: Golf Club, Sports Center, Sky Rink, Roller Rinks, Field House, AMC Cineplex, Chelsea Piers Bowling and a Maritime Center.

The 150,000 sq. ft. Sports Center includes the world's longest indoor running track and the largest rock-climbing wall in the northeast. It also features gigantic cardio-vascular and strength training facilities. In addition, the

Sports Center offers league play, wellness seminars, sports specific training and spa service. Track and field events can be accommodated in the 18,000 sq. ft. flexible infield as well as volleyball, touch football, and special events. There is a six lane, 25 yard long swimming pool, two aerobics studios, three basketball courts and 13,000 sq. ft. of locker room facilities: steam rooms, saunas and massage areas.

The Sky Rink is NY's only year round, indoor ice skating rink. There are two rinks, a pro shop, skate rental and a Famous Famiglia Cafe as well as four lounges that can be rented for special occasions. There is seating for about 1600 including two sky boxes and a 6,000 sq. ft. sun deck (The Beach Club) with its own bar and food service.

The Roller Rinks feature the only two regulation-sized, professionally surfaced "in-line" and roller skating rinks in Manhattan. The Field House, an 80,000 sq. ft. space, houses a 23,000 sq. ft. gymnastic training center; a rock climbing wall for children; two basketball courts and two artificial turf fields which can be used for indoor soccer, field hockey and lacrosse. The facility also accommodates a toddler gym, four dance studios/party rooms and two mezzanines one of which is for spectators.

The 1000 sq. ft. practice putting green and 52 weather protected and heated driving stalls on four levels are only some of the attractions of The Golf Club at Pier 59. The Golf Academy is a 2000 sq. ft. indoor learning center and there is also a 200 yard artificial turf runway and four custom target greens by Target Greens

Inc. Besides locker rooms and a Reebok Golf Shop, there is the Chelsea Brewing Co. which is a popular waterfront restaurant brewery.

The redevelopments of these four surviving piers marks a major step in the rebirth of Manhattan's waterfront for public use, recreation and as an entertainment destination. According to Paul Greenberger, writing in the New York Times, "It is a good work of design, full of a recognition of the potential of this unusual 30 acre site. The place has a presence, a presence that makes it like no other place in New York." Alex Williams, describing this complex in The New York Magazine said, "It's so user friendly, so open and primary-color happy, it radiates optimism." ∎

ALL AMERICAN SPORTPARK

Las Vegas, NV

Architectural Design
Swisher & Hall, Las Vegas, NV

Photography
Jeffrey Greene Photography, Las Vegas

All American SportPark is a multi-use, sports themed retail and entertainment complex in Las Vegas which many consider the "Themed Entertainment Capitol" of the world. Located on a 65 acre park, the 96,000 sq. ft. indoor pavilion is a focal draw to natives and tourists alike in search of a different kind of entertainment. Included in this complex is the All Sports Arena with "in-line" skating and roller rink, a rock climbing wall, miniature golf course, putting range, billiards and darts, sports themed photography studio, a game arcade plus retail shops, restaurant and sports bar.

Located on the sprawling park designed by Swisher & Hall of Las Vegas are the Slugger Stadium which is equipped with batting cages modeled after those used in Major League baseball stadiums; a Nascar Speedpark with three go-kart tracks with cars designed for children and adults; and a nine hole, championship par-three golf course. All American Sports is the first enclave of its kind to bring together Nascar, Major League Baseball Properties, Callaway Golf and Pepsi in one complex.

Swisher & Hall designed this facility to provide Las Vegas with a family oriented, non-gaming activity center. As in their other projects, the architectural firm has remained firmly grounded in exploring "The High Desert Design": establishing a relationship between the built and the natural environment. The layout of the vast park and the building designs continue the firm's practice. "Building design, environmental response, functionalism, and cost effectiveness are also critical factors in developing sustaining buildings which support these design goals." ∎

OAKLAND
ICE CENTER

Oakland, CA

Architectural Design
Bottom Duvivier, Redwood City, CA

Principal in Charge
John Duvivier

Project Designer
John Spotorno

Project Manager
Bill Larsen

Architect
Andrew Chien

The Oakland Ice Center sits on one city block of 90,000 sq. ft. in downtown Oakland across from the landmark Fox Theater. This area is re-emerging as Oakland's Entertainment District.

The challenge was to maintain the "grand mass of an urban public building" yet down-size the scale to create a more inviting and friendly presence in the streetscape. The designers broke both of the street elevations into separate identities through the use of different materials and by shifting the building plan. This also defines the two different rinks inside.

One side of the facade is sheathed in a natural, galvanized, horizontally corrugated metal siding while the other side is finished in a smooth, more refined, white metal panel siding. Creating a "durable human scale street elevation" are the eight foot high patterned glazed masonry walls upon which both systems rest. A large brightly colored, two story high curved canopy links the two sides together and creates "a large inviting entrance and highlights the creative architecture inside." The banners that add color accents to the facade feature work of local artists.

Inside, a dynamically angled yellow wall is broken up with areas of glass. Through these, the viewer can see into the cafe and the Pro Shop, both important to the economic health of the Ice Center. The design assists the traffic movement since between the free skating sessions there can be as many as 300 people trying to get in while another 300 are trying to get out.

One of the rinks is built to Olympic specifications and the other can accommodate NHL hockey. According to John Duvivier of the Bottom Duvivier architectural firm, "Keeping the ice hard and the people comfortable remains a contradiction. We used glass barriers in the cafe and the Pro Shop and the observa-

tion areas to separate the heating zones and keep utility bills low." In addition, there is a "core" area with ten locker rooms, a skate rental and repair facility, an aerobics/dance/warm-up room, a weight room, a snack bar and bleacher seating for about 1800. The project had a modest budget, a tight schedule and definitely required abuse resistant materials. Bottom Duvivier resorted to economical materials used in an imaginative mix of colors and patterns and in finishes "that heighten the festive spirit of the building" at minimal cost.

Kristi Yamiguchi, The Olympic medalist ice skater said, "This rink is a great opportunity to bring people together and to get kids involved in sports." ■

EXTREME FITNESS

Toronto, ON, Canada

Design
ll X lV Design Associates, Toronto, ON

Photography
David Whittaker, Toronto, ON

The challenge presented to ll X lV Design Associates of Toronto was to create a state-of-the-art health club that would be beautiful as well as functional and the fitness environment would be as enjoyable as possible.

The site is a 27,000 sq. ft., long abandoned warehouse in a suburban industrial mall. Part of the design initiative was to create an ambience that would prove "welcoming, well organized and security conscious so that neighboring families with small children as well as trendy singles would sign up." The designers added large industrial style windows to break up the monolithic facade and also allow daylight to penetrate the building. To de-emphasize the vastness of the full service facility, the designers created "pockets of space": from locker room areas to the splash pool. Each one is a "perfect and personable setting." All areas beyond the lobby have access controls and there are

separate change areas for men, women, boys and girls.

A catwalk-like mezzanine was built on the perimeter of the second story aerobics studio to provide an interesting view of the cardiovascular equipment in use. In the large machine rooms, full mirrored walls were banished along with cold fluorescent. The lighting is now soft and flattering and more human-scale, individual mirrors are supplied. All lighting now is incandescent and accent lamps are used in key areas like reception, evaluation and in the sales center. Indirect wall washers highlight the texture of the concrete block walls while adding color and also softening the look of the material. The designers, for practical purposes used "indestructible" materials such as concrete block and slate but they eased the overall effect with warm earth tones like tan, ocher, warm gray, cream and moss green. A brilliant deep blue color, picked up from the tiles in the

swimming pool, is repeated in the large elliptical columns and in the water image artwork chosen for the surrounding area. To add interest throughout, natural wood details were added along with compelling photographic works of art "to add a sophisticated but personal touch."

The ll X lV designed millwork includes a 40 ft. main service counter, sound system cabinets and cocktail tables and stools in the waiting room. To provide privacy for the sales area, the designers created a metal framed mullion and glass panel system. Today, the functionally finished yet refined facility has "a lively, friendly atmosphere where members can relax, meet friends and get into the best shapes in their lives." ■

BUS WELLNESS CENTER

Santa Monica, CA

Design
Steven Ehrlich Architects, Culver City, CA

Principals
Steven Ehrlich & Nick Seierup

Project Architect
James Schmidt

Project Team
Iris Anna Regn/Supachai Kiatkwankul/Gary Alonza/Markus Hintzen/Sookja Lee/Mei Ting Lin

Photography
Courtesy of Steven Ehrlich Architects

Using a tight budget and working within the 5000 sq. ft. confines of a former Greyhound Bus Terminal on Fifth St. in Santa Monica, Steven Ehrlich Architects turned the unused space into a prize winning design for the Bus Wellness Center: a new concept in health, fitness and training.

The original 1950s facade was restored to reveal the structures "good bones" and modernized with galvanized steel and paint. The elevation along Fifth St. was stripped back to reveal the tapered steel frame, a light diffusing screen and then "opened up to reemphasize the roadside visibility of the inherent form." By removing three partitions, a central space was carved out of the interior to allow entry from Fifth St. and the parking lot behind. Here is located the greeting/check-in desk, the juice/coffee and vitamin bar and a retail sales shop. Architectural forms direct the traffic into the personalized weightlifting training area, a cardio and dance room, and the locker and shower facilities. To bring light and air in, the architects reproduced the original street windows and also added some skylights

Wherever possible, the existing building's material was reused. The designers had the brick walls sandblasted, the steel framing painted and they added drywall partitions over the existing terrazzo flooring in the waiting room. New partitions were painted in bright colors to play off of the existing walls. Walls which were infill within existing walls were sheathed in stained oriented strand board and galvanized steel. Where sections of flooring had to be removed to put in new wiring and/or for plumbing lines, these were infilled with dyed concrete which was also used as a leveling compound throughout the project.

A new graphic program was also designed which "plays slender new corporate identity elements off against the existing 'Bus' signage which was retailed for its associative memory purposes." ∎

154

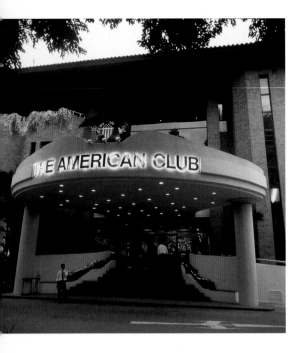

ACS FITNESS CENTER

Singapore

Design
**David B. Tokiwa & Assoc. PTE, Ltd.,
Singapore**

Photography
Courtesy David B. Tokiwa

Singapore is where East meets West and it is also where much of the trade and finance of the Pacific Rim is conducted. The American Club, in Singapore, is often the "home away from home" for many U.S. business executives and statespersons whose work brings them to this part of the world. At The American Club they find the things that they are familiar with and also the people who share similar experiences.

The Fitness Center, shown here, and the Spa are only two of the special areas in the club that are frequented destinations. The project, designed by the Singapore firm of David B. Tokiwa & Associates, Pte, Ltd. is fresh, clean and contemporary. Light, native woods from Malaysia and Indonesia are used to provide the

American concept of "warmth and friendliness" that the guests look for and these are balanced with a light neutral palette and an attractive and stimulating light plan.

Sweeping curves define the reception area and the towel storage area. The arced dropped ceiling panels reinforce the line of the desk while the angled vertical posts add a dynamic quality to the design of the space. There are areas in each work-out space filled with multi-TV monitors that serve as a source of entertainment as well as a distraction for the members toiling at the state-of-the-art equipment. The floors in the fitness areas are paved with a light colored native stone. ∎

TROCADERO

Piccadilly Circus, London, UK

Design
RTKL, Ltd., London

Photography:
Nancy Robinson Watson

The historic 500,000 sq. ft. Piccadilly Circus landmark, in the heart of London's entertainment zone, has been renewed, renovated and reenergized by the architectural design magic of RTKL's U.K. branch office. Paul Hanegraaf, VP and managing director of RTKL-UK, Ltd. said, "At the Trocadero, emerging technologies, futuristic design and theming, leisure and retail come together to create a 21st century urban entertainment envi-

ronment that is unique to Europe and unlike any other to be found in most of the world today." What the designers have created here is a high tech environment that offers a sequence of experiences that visitors will long remember.

Included in the seven story structure are Virtual World, Virgin Cinemas, an HMV Superstore, Showscan's Emaginator, Planet Hollywood and a 100,000 sq. ft. SegaWorld virtual reality theme park on the upper levels. Trocadero also boasts of London's first 3D Imax cinema: a 300-seat theater with a 50 ft. by 70 ft. screen and the latest in sound and visual technology. Using storyboard techniques, similar to those used in movie making, an overall theme was created and RTKL

developed an "intergalactic transit station" within the central atrium. The centerpiece of the design is the vertical transportation system—the "rocket" escalator that transports visitors up through the 125 ft. atrium—past the 108 screen, wraparound video wall and the multimedia columns that broadcast sound, light and lasers. Live action cameras and colored moving spotlights close in as guests pierce a massive curved projection screen to arrive at the entrance to SegaWorld—all in 107 seconds! The futuristic theme is enhanced by a multimedia show that is scheduled for every 30 minutes. Encompassing film and theater and reinforced with state-of-the-art audiovisuals, lasers and lights, the show features T-Roc, the Trocadero mascot. T-Roc

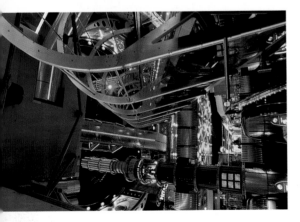

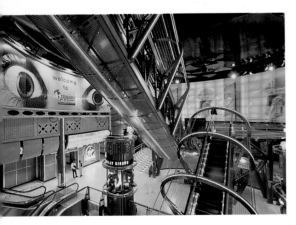

also figures prominently in the graphic details of the project and is an effective marketing icon.

The atmosphere of Trocadero can be completely controlled and "reprogrammed." Thus, it can be changed to appeal to children and parents during the daylight hours and then take on a different attitude for the slightly older demographic group that fills the space at night. According to Paul Hanegraaf, "The success of the new Trocadero illustrates that entertainment is a powerful and potent development component." ■

ENTERTAINMENT CENTER AT IRVINE SPECTRUM

Irvine, CA

Design
RTKL, Los Angeles, CA

VP in charge
Paul F. Jacob, AIA

Project Manager
Dave Schmitz

VP in Charge of Environmental Graphics
Katie J. Sprague

Environmental Graphics Project Designer
Kevin N.Horn

Photography
David Whitcomb Baltmore, MD

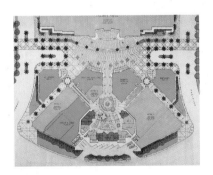

The Entertainment Complex at Irvine Spectrum is organized around a central plaza and the 270,000 sq.ft. center "becomes a vibrant, animated space for shopping and enjoyment." Organized in the Pleasure Zone is a 21 screen Edwards Cinema of 110,000 sq. ft. and a 400-seat Oasis food court, themed restaurants and a multitude of retail operations.

This area is Phase ll of the Irvine Spectrum and it not only continues the entertainment opportunities afforded in the original phase but has extended it to fun places like Dave & Busters, Gameworks, and NASCAR Silicon Motor Speedway. The first phase drew on a Moroccan Bazaar theme while this new area is designed as a "stylized version of the Alhambra in Granada Spain." Though based on the thirteenth century citadel which is considered the epitome of Moorish architecture, according to the RTKL designers/architects, "the architecture is intended to drive home the theme of fun, relaxation and enjoyment." Paul Jacob, VP and managing director of 10-8—RTKL's entertainment design studio—says, "We've remained pretty true to the quality of spaces. We took the plan of the Alhambra—actually took those existing spaces and rearranged them in a differ-

ent procession." The layout includes the Alhambra-inspired Court of Lions which features a fountain with colored arcades and giant palms and the Court of Myrtles—complete with reflecting pool, arching jets of water, arcades and seating areas. A bell tower of over 90 feet is the high point in the complex and it is located in the Court of Dorado. The three courts are linked by "souks," native, bazaar-like shopping streets with overhead trellises and hanging awnings.

Beyond the variety of permanent attractions, the Entertainment Center features an on-going program of thematic special events and activities geared to a wide variety of interests and ages.

Edwards 21 Cinema is located in this book in the cinema section. ■

DENVER PAVILIONS

Denver, CO

Design/Architecture
**ELS/Elbasani & Logan Architects,
Los Angeles, CA**

Principal in Charge
Barry Elbasani, FAIA

Project Manager
D.Jamie Rusin

Design Team
**Paul Anziani/Laura Blake, AIA/Kelly
Johnson/Gary Logsdon/Gerald
Navarro/Vince Taboada**

Lighting
George Sexton Assoc.

Photography
Andrew Kramer, Denver

The newest, most colorful and certainly most entertaining addition to Denver's downtown is the Denver Pavilions located on the open air shopping area on the 16th St. Mall. The 354,000 sq. ft. pavilions occupies two blocks and the "active and luminous buildings are a retail beacon for the entire Denver area."

The architects/designers, ELS/Elbasani & Logan Architects respected the existing scale and fabric of the nearby historic buildings when they designed the facade. "Within the contextual structure, transparent walls offer the pedestrians a look into the next century, with a rare and dynamic assembly of entertainment uses made visible." Restaurants and shops tenant the first two levels while the third level is occupied by a 15-screen cinema and several night clubs. During the day, the shops and cafes welcome the city's working population with the landscaped plazas and shaded arcades. At night, people are drawn to this downtown entertainment Mecca by the colorful glow that emanates from the curved structures. Some of the tenants that bring in the shoppers and the entertainment seekers are:Niketown, Hard Rock Cafe, Wolfgang Puck's Cafe, Virgin Megastore, Banana Republic, The Gap and—of course—the United Artists multiplex cinema. There are two below ground levels of parking that can accommodate 800 vehicles and an additional 6500 spaces are also available within a two block radius.

The strength of the Denver Pavilions is its "Trinity of Synergy" and these are entertainment, dining and shopping. "The synergy is what occurs when all three are placed in one setting," said Steve Raabe, the Denver Post's business writer. "The result, the theory goes, is a powerhouse, a juggernaut that draws customers from farther away and empties their wallets faster than any mere suburban mall."

As in some of the other entertainment venues we have featured, this development is helping to revitalize an urban downtown sector. ∎

DENVER PAVILIONS
Denver Pavilions Limited Partnership
ELS/Elbasani & Logan Architects

PACIFIC PLACE

Seattle, WA.

Design/Architecture
NBBJ, Seattle, WA. and Elkus Manfredi, Boston, MA

Photography
J. Fred Housel / Steve Keating, Seattle, WA

The five story retail/entertainment complex, Pacific Place, is situated in downtown Seattle. The 335,000 sq. ft. shopping/dining/going-out center is "a world alive with the pulse of a city and culture unique to the Pacific Northwest."

The centerpiece of the complex is a soaring, crescent shaped atrium topped with a 12,500 sq. ft. skylight that allows daylight to flood the interior space. At night, the lamp lights that illuminate Pacific Place add the feeling of a European plaza. Throughout, the architects/designers, a joint venture of Elkus Manfredi of Boston and NBBJ of Seattle, stressed the outdoor ambience through their use of textures, materials and colors. The flooring is textured concrete, the steel is painted and the region's traditional use of timber is reflected in the extensive use of cherry and vertical grain fir.

The designers, working with the retailers, developed an exterior that "expresses the character of the individual stores." An articulated facade, by breaking down the size of the city block building, gives the impression of a collection of smaller, separate retail buildings. It "maintains a scale that is not overwhelming to its neighbors."

Pacific Place is home to an 11-screen, 3100-seat cinema complex, several top rated restaurants and brand name retailers like Tiffany, Max Mara, Cartier, J.Peterman, Club Monaco, J.Crew and Pottery Barn. A six level, underground parking facility can accommodate up to 1200 vehicles. ∎

BEALE STREET

Memphis, TN

Concept
John Elkington, Performa Enterprises

Photography
Courtesy of Performa Enterprises

I n 1983 the Tennessee legislators passed a bill that made it possible to restore and rejuvenate Beale St.: "The Crossroads of America's Music." The new law allowed the purchaser of an alcoholic drink to legally carry that drink on Beale Street—anywhere from 2nd and 4th Sts. This ruling made it possible to bring life and fun back to Beale St. where people can now move freely from club to club and from band to band, and on festival weekends thousands come out to enjoy the music and spirit of that street in a stimulating and neighborly environment. Another important ruling, that year, made it legal for Beale St. businesses to remain open on Sunday.

The Beale Street Management, now known as Performa Entertainment Real Estate, inc. took over and presided at the rebirth of Beale Street as a viable entertainment destination. John Elkington, of Beale St. Management said, "Over the past three years, the Beale Street historic district has been transformed from a decaying string of buildings to an emerging entertainment center. Commerce has returned to the street, the street has developed a new spirit and it has once again become the Mecca for musicians." Richard Hackett, the Mayor of Memphis, adds, "Beale Street represents the very best of our city's proud musical heritage. The street's restoration is nearly finished and we can already feel, hear and see the difference. Great things are happening on Beale Street."

Today the street is alive with flashing neon signs, music soaring and mingling with the happy street sounds pouring out of clubs, restaurants, bars and retail establishments. It all celebrates the resurrection of a neighborhood.

Promoting the musical heritage is the key factor in maintaining its unique look and for attracting visitors and jazz-lovers from all over the world. W.C.Handy's Memphis home has been relocated to the corner of Beale St. and Fourth. It has been restored and now serves as a "blues" museum filled with memorabilia of the composer and his music. Memphis music greats are commemorated with brass plaques on Beale Street's Walk of Fame. Among those honored are Elvis Presley, Memphis Slim and B.B.King. In Handy Park, a monument honoring Rufus Thomas has been installed and to tell the vivid story of Beale Street's history there are historical markers set up along the street.

It is hoped that the revival of this area in downtown Memphis will also serve as a stimulant to the rest of the southern end of the downtown district. "The entire downtown area, in addition to Beale Street, is blossoming into an entertainment district," says John Elkington. "Lots of restaurants have opened and we could support a lot more. The best is yet to come." ■

CLARKE QUAY, ENTERTAINMENT CENTRE

Singapore

Design
ELS, Elbasani & Logan, Architects, Los Angeles, CA

Design Team
Carol Shen, AIA/Alex Achimore/Cheryl Morgan AIA/Al Costa/David Fawcett/Avery Taylor Moore

Associate Architect
RSP Architects, Singapore

Photography
Dixi Carrillo, Trends, Int.

The Los Angeles based architectural firm of Elbasani & Logan (ELS) won an international competition and thus the contract to restore and improve a five block long district located along the Singapore River. The new design included the restoration and rehasbbing of existing century or more old warehouses and "shophouses" into a vital and exciting retail/restaurant/entertainment destination.

The challenge, from the start, was for ELS to adapt the old structures to current viable uses without compromising their original character. The design team determined that the facades, roofs, materials, detailing, airwells (enclosed with skylights) and covered walkways were the most significant architectural features. Some of the structures were in serious disrepair and needed more than "cosmetic" renovation: they needed complete reconstruction. While modern materials and construction materials were employed, the ornaments, finishes and colors were based on historic precedent. To reinforce the landmark character, a broad palette of muted and variegated colors were selected so that the project would look "restored" rather than "new."

Incorporated into the plan was a new, five story parking facility that was "sympathetic in design and scale" and two new buildings were added along River Valley Road. Here articulated plaster facades, timber screens and windows, recessed arcades and iron gates were used in a contemporary interpretation of the scale and character of the neighboring historic buildings. These buildings contain almost 200, air-conditioned, shops, bars and restaurants. There is also a scaled down bumboat ride and a high tech presentation that combines animated cartoon characters, lighting and special effects to tell the 200 year history of the Singapore River.

Along the water the emphasis is on the variety of dining experiences. The design recalls "the riverfront's heyday with broad shaded streets, authentic gas lamps, food stalls and restored tongkangs (barges) that now serve as dining pavilions." ∎

The Visual
Reference
Library

of Architecture and Design

Visit

www.visualreference.com